PUB WALK

The Wayfarer's Walk

Other areas covered in the Pub Walks series include:

A complete catalogue is available from the publisher at
3 Catherine Road, Newbury, Berkshire.

PUB WALKS ALONG

The Wayfarer's Walk

TWENTY CIRCULAR WALKS

Barry Shurlock

COUNTRYSIDE BOOKS
NEWBURY, BERKSHIRE

First published 1996
© Barry Shurlock 1996

COUNTRYSIDE BOOKS
3 Catherine Road
Newbury, Berkshire

ISBN 1 85306 413 0

'I like this pub,' said Capt'n Rog.

Designed by Mon Mohan
Maps and pub photographs by the author
Other photographs by Sally Bowman

Produced through MRM Associates Ltd., Reading
Printed by Woolnough Bookbinding Ltd., Irthlingborough

Contents

Publisher's Note

We hope that you obtain considerable enjoyment from this book; great care has been taken in its preparation. However, changes of landlord and actual closures are sadly not uncommon. Likewise, although at the time of publication all routes followed public rights of way or permitted paths, diversion orders can be made and permissions withdrawn.

We cannot of course be held responsible for such diversion orders and any inaccuracies in the text which result from these or any other changes to the routes nor any damage which might result from walkers trespassing on private property. We are anxious though that all details covering the walks and the pubs are kept up to date and would therefore welcome information from readers which would be relevant to future editions.

WW The Wayfarer's Walk – Overall route from Inkpen Beacon, Berkshire to Emsworth, Hampshire.

The Wayfarer's Walk
THE ROUTE

Introduction

It is hardly surprising that pub walks have become one of the most popular forms of leisure for a large number of people in Britain. The pub and the countryside are, after all, two of the country's greatest assets. This book is one of a series that covers pub walks related to a particular long-distance trail – in this case, the Wayfarer's Walk. This covers a distance of 70 miles, from Inkpen Beacon on the Berkshire–Hampshire border in the north to Emsworth, in the south. At first it runs along the Inkpen and North Hants Ridgeway, with its magnificent views, then heads down the Candover valley and across the hills to the Meon valley. It winds its way across to Hambledon, the cradle of cricket, and then drops down to the head of Langstone Harbour and so on to Emsworth, which lies on the edge of Chichester Harbour. The 20 walks included in this book explore some of the best reaches of the trail.

There are several good reasons for basing a series of circular walks on a long-distance trail such as the Wayfarer's Walk. A great deal of thought has been given to devising these trails and they therefore cover some of the best walking country in any particular area. Some walkers want to 'sample' a long-distance trail, rather than setting off on a marathon. They may be encouraged to try the whole trail, they may not: this book will give them the chance to decide.

The walks in this book are spread along the length of the trail, though obviously they have been restricted by the existence or otherwise of a decent pub! Equally, they are intended to be circular, which has required some ingenuity in some cases and a good honest fudge in others. Footpaths often fail to honour this need for circularity and in some cases the resulting walks are not completely circular, or are somewhat longer than I would have wished. In some cases I have given a short cut for those whose feet are feeling the pinch, or are otherwise disposed to a shorter route.

Most of the pubs mentioned in this book have been in business for so long that no one knows when they started. However, during the planning stages for the walks two pubs that I had intended including went on the market as 'going concern or private residence'. So, on the principle of 'use it or lose it', I suggest that walkers are generous in their food orders!

Each walk starts with a description of the pub and its facilities. This was done in the knowledge that things change . . . landlords change, menus change, beers change, but the overall character of a pub may go on. This information will give the walker some idea of what to expect, for some pubs have in essence stayed the same for as long as I can remember. What I have written is mostly based on what the landlord or landlady told me. I have not therefore compiled a critical 'good pub' guide, though I would be proud to take a maiden aunt or a gourmet great-uncle into most of them. Talking to publicans has made me realise what a good-natured lot they are and how keen they are to provide what the customer wants. A tidal wave of real ales and home-cooked foods has jerked the English pub from the pre-packaged 'fizzy beer' rut into which it had generally sunk.

As regard matters of pub policy, particularly concerning walkers, I have found most publicans very understanding. For example, all of them were generous in their attitudes towards the use of the pub's car park, provided the walker patronises the bar. No reader, I am sure, needs reminding that it does all walkers a great disservice to park the car at the pub, go for a walk and then leave without patronising the bar. Incredibly, some people do just that. It is a simple courtesy to ask the barman for permission to park and to ask where would be most convenient. One landlord told me of the day when somebody parked over the cellar delivery hatch and then walked off . . . on delivery day!

Another matter in which the views of the landlord need respecting is that of 'own sandwiches'. Can they be eaten with a drink in the garden or not? Most said yes, but not all. Once again, it's surely better to ask than to fumble around in a paper bag beneath the table (though most of us must have done it!). As regards dogs, in the opinion of most publicans (and Health and Safety officials) they and food don't mix, though some pubs have a foodless snug where dogs can sit happily on a lead and others will provide a bowl of water if left outside. On the question of muddy boots, it is common sense to slip them off, or ask if there is a bar with a tiled floor where boots are acceptable. Finally, relatively recent changes in the law now mean that many pubs stay open all day, particularly over summer weekends. This must be the greatest advance in civilisation that has come the way of the walker for a long time!

The main description of the walk has deliberately been kept simple. I could have written a great deal on the background of the walks, but in the interests of space confined myself to straightforward and, I hope, clear directions. Most of these walks were undertaken in late 1995 and early 1996. No doubt some features that have been described will change, but I have tried to bear this in mind and have therefore erred on the side of giving too much information rather than too little. It is, of course, always possible to get lost, but if you take an Ordnance Survey map, and follow the walk directions carefully you are unlikely to get very lost. One piece of equipment that I always carry is a compass. It may seem over the top in the gentle countryside of southern England, but it does, for example, enable choices to be made between seemingly identical paths. More importantly, it can be used to navigate across crop fields belonging to farmers who selfishly plough right across public footpaths. In my opinion they ought to be heavily fined. But meanwhile, use your compass and boldly go through crop fields where you are sure there is a right of way – it's another 'use it or lose it' issue. In most cases where the walk goes across the middle of a crop field I have given a course in degrees magnetic (which is about 5 degrees more than the true course, i.e. the course according to the map).

The sketch maps that accompany each pub walk are intended to provide a simple guide to the walk. They also show that part of the walk (sometimes a very small part) which coincides with a leg of the Wayfarer's Walk. It should be possible to follow the pub walk with the aid of these maps, but you should also carry a copy of the relevant Ordnance Survey map, which is specified in the text above the main walk directions.

Below the walk directions for a particular pub walk there is, in most cases, a short description of the leg of the Wayfarer's Walk that links this walk with the next one. This is not intended to provide enough information with which to navigate the Wayfarer's Walk, though the trail is very well signposted and the experienced walker should have no trouble in following it, provided he carries the appropriate Ordnance Survey maps. Because many people no longer use the English yard as a unit of distance, I have used metres. Traditionalists may care to remind themselves that 100 metres is equal to 108 yards.

Finally, a few comments on walking in general. Each walker no doubt has his own views on the best clothes to wear and the most appropriate equipment to carry. I have my own checklist which I consult before leaving the house. Depending on the season, it caters for the insults of heat and cold, rain and sun. It reminds me that binoculars and a compass are useful, that plasters and antiseptic cream are no bad thing and that a forked stick will help me up and down hills. All this (not the stick!) is bundled into a very small rucksack, together with a change or two of socks and second mode of footwear. I try not to carry food or drink, though I often take an apple. And I always take some cash; not many pubs still give credit these days!

Responding immediately to any discomfort in the foot region (or elsewhere!) is a good rule for the walker. I also try to compensate immediately for being too hot or too cold. Simple manoeuvres enable the heat of the body to be controlled like the central heating system it is. For example, reversing a jacket and holding it across the chest as you meet a headwind is likely to be more effective than putting on another layer and breaking out in a sweat. Regular walkers will not need to read this sort of stuff; indeed, I would welcome hearing about their own pet techniques. Happy walking! Happy tippling! Happy eating!

Barry Shurlock
Summer 1996

Key for Pub Walk maps

→ → → →   Pub Walk

··· → ··· →   Pub Walk along Wayfarer's Walk

· · · · · · · · · ·   Wayfarer's Walk

▬▬▬▬▬   Road

═-═-═-═-═   Track

▬ ▬ ▬ ▬ ▬ ▬   Footpath

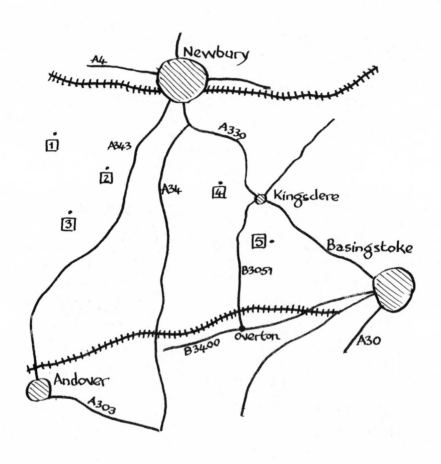

Map showing the location of Pub Walks 1–5

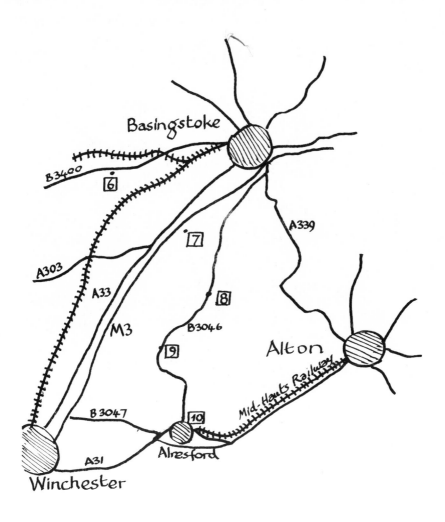

Map showing the location of Pub Walks 6–10

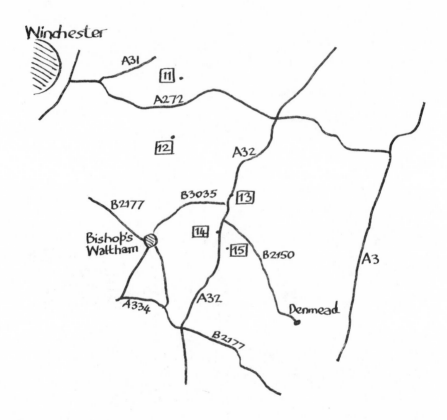

Map showing the location of Pub Walks 11–15

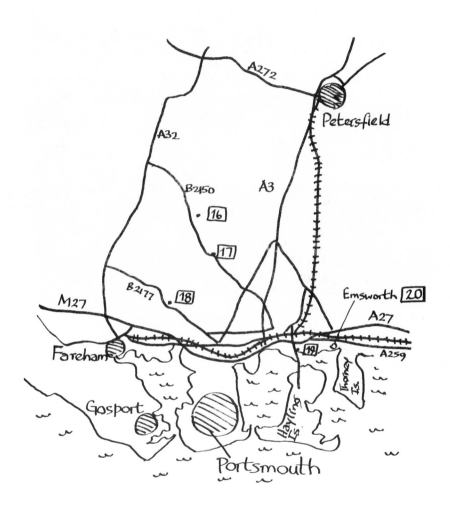

Map showing the location of Pub Walks 16–20

[1] Inkpen
The Crown and Garter

This freehouse is on the edge of Inkpen proper, in an area called Inkpen Common. It is so deep in the country that the barman is used to people coming in looking lost (not walkers, of course!). It dates from the 16th century and is thought to have been a staging post. It has a single large oak-beamed bar with a welcome open fire. There is also an area with a pool table, fruit machines and Sky television.

The menu is good basic pub grub, with T-bone steaks for the ravenous. Real ales include Hampshire Lionheart and Arkells Village Bitter and there is also a draught cider. There is a large garden outside with a play area for children. Genuine walkers are welcome to eat their sandwiches in the garden, provided they have bought drinks. Well-behaved dogs are welcome outside meal times.

Opening hours are from 12 noon to 3 pm and 6 pm to 11 pm on weekdays and Saturday and 12 noon to 10.30 pm on summer Sundays. Meals are served from 12 noon to 2.30 pm at lunchtime and between 7 pm and 9.30 pm in the evenings.

Telephone: 01488 668325.

How to get there: Inkpen Common is situated about a mile south-east of Inkpen village, which is itself about 4 miles south-east of Hungerford.

Parking: The pub has a good-sized car park.

Length of the walk: 4 miles (with a shorter version of 2 miles indicated). Map: OS Landranger 174 Newbury and Wantage (inn GR 378638).

The walk rises up onto the Inkpen Ridgeway, which is followed for about 15 miles by the Wayfarer's Walk, with exceptional views to the north. The route only includes a short section of the long-distance route, but gives a flavour of its 'highlands' stretch en route to Emsworth and Langstone Harbour. It is the only walk in Berkshire in the book.

The Walk
From the Crown and Garter take a track running alongside its garden fence in a south-easterly direction. After about 500 metres the track passes houses on the left-hand side and further on emerges onto a country road. Turn right onto the road and after 500 metres, where the road turns sharply to the right (Point A on the sketch map; if a shorter walk is required, turn right here), take a footpath that continues ahead along the edge of a copse in a south-westerly direction. To the left is a crop field and ahead the ridgeway. The footpath passes an old quarry and then the field boundary takes a sharp turn to the left. Here our route turns right into a copse and soon comes to a minor road at a junction. We turn left onto the road, signed to Faccombe and Ashmansworth, which climbs steeply onto West Woodhay Down. At the top of the rise the **wxw** Wayfarer's Walk comes in from the right and continues along the road to a T-junction. We leave the long-distance path at this point and turn left along a byway signed: 'no through route for vehicles'.

After 300 metres a bridleway comes in from the left. The road falls for about another 300 metres and is then crossed by a bridleway at a point where Berkshire touches Hampshire. Here we turn left onto the bridleway and continue towards Highwood Farm on the right. Just before reaching the access drive to the farm, the

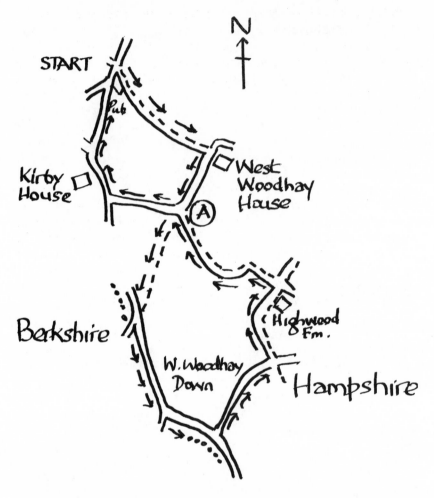

route turns left on a track that runs in a north-westerly direction. It winds round to emerge at Point A above. Just before reaching this point the waters of the lake belonging to West Woodhay House can be seen in the distance on the right-hand side. From Point A, turn left onto a minor road and then right at a T-junction after about 500 metres. This leads back to the Crown and Garter. The route falls between steep banks to Kirby House on the left, a lovely five-bay country house. Just beyond the house a road forks off to the right and climbs back to Inkpen Common and the pub.

WW The Wayfarer's Walk – Combe Gibbet to Upper Eastwick Copse (2½ miles)

The Wayfarer's Walk starts in Berkshire at Combe Gibbet on the summit of Inkpen Beacon. The first gibbet on this site probably dates from the 17th century, though it has been replaced on several occasions. The present modern replica of the original stands on an enormous Neolithic barrow. The route of the first part of the Wayfarer's Walk keeps to the ridgeway that falls steeply to the north, down to the river Kennet. There are wonderful views from these high lands, which once formed a natural boundary between Hampshire and Berkshire, until legislation of 1882 moved Combe into Berkshire. It passes across Walbury Hill, at 297 metres the highest chalk down in England, and the site of a massive hillfort covering more than 80 acres. It then passes West Woodhay Down, which is included in this walk from the Crown and Garter. It continues along the ridge, past Upper Eastwick copse, which takes us to Pub Walk 2.

[2] East End
The Axe and Compasses

This is a rare example of a real village pub that concentrates on good beer and good food at very reasonable prices. It is said to have always been a pub, at least for the last 400 years, and always with the same name ... well almost. It used to be the Adze and Compasses, until people forgot what an adze was. And the compasses are the sort used for drawing, not a ship's compass, so presumably the name has something to do with the woodworker's craft.

The oak-beamed main bar has a cheerful open fire and a darts and pool area at one end. To the right is the dining room (deliberately not called a restaurant), where good home-cooked food is on offer. To the rear of the pub there is a patio where one's own food can be eaten with a drink. Dogs are welcome in the bar, almost more welcome than the customers! There is cider on draught and the real ales on offer include Wadworth 6X, Hook Norton Bitter and Bass. There are well chosen, reasonably priced white and red wines.

The opening times are, Monday, evening only 6 pm to 11 pm; Tuesday to Saturday, 12 noon to 2.30 pm (or later) and 6 pm to

11 pm, and Sunday, 12 noon to 3.30 pm and 7 pm to 10.30 pm. Meals are available from 12 noon to 2 pm, and 7 pm to 9.30 pm except Sunday evenings.

Telephone: 01635 253403.

How to get there: East End is about 6 miles south-west of Newbury. From the A343 Newbury to Andover road it is reached by turning west to Woolton Hill, 2 miles before reaching Highclere. East End lies a mile to the west of Woolton Hill and is signed.

Parking: There is a car park at the back of the pub.

Length of the walk: 5 miles. Map: OS Landranger 174 Newbury and Wantage (inn GR 415614).

The challenge of this walk can be seen from East End village (nothing less like the East End can be imagined!) – it is the North Hampshire Ridgeway, which gives such drama to the countryside hereabouts. The walk starts off in pleasant farmland and soon climbs up to the ridge, which it follows for almost a mile, before descending back to the plain. It winds back through the village of East Woodhay, past grand houses and the church.

The Walk

Opposite the Axe and Compasses a fingerpost points south along a footpath that leads to a stile with farm buildings beyond. Leaving the farm buildings on the right, the path crosses another stile and follows the right-hand side of the field to another stile. It continues through a crop field in a south-westerly direction (220° magnetic) to a fingerpost alongside a track. The footpath continues at another fingerpost on the other side of the track and crosses a field diagonally. After 200 metres it meets another track (a byway) on a bend. The route continues ahead, along the track, towards the North Hants Ridgeway, past East Woodhay Reservoir (Southern Water). The track winds under huge beech trees as it climbs to the ridge to meet an old deep-cut road at a fingerpost. Here the route turns left and after 300 metres cuts back to the right along a **WW** bridleway. You are now on the Wayfarer's Walk. The walk continues along the ridge for about 1,500 metres, with

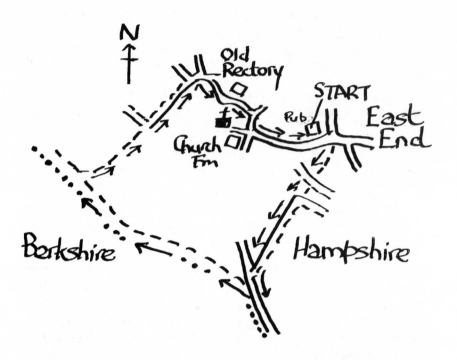

wonderful views to the north. Just beyond a house set in woods on the left, the track dog-legs left and right. Further on the bridleway runs along the Hampshire–Berkshire border, which stretches south in a tongue of land that includes Inkpen and Combe. The path passes through a small copse (Upper Eastwick) and, after descending for a few hundred metres, near a field gate, reaches a signed bridleway that turns back to the right. Here we leave the Wayfarer's Walk.

The bridleway continues through a galvanised iron gate in a fence and then falls steeply to a wooden gate. This descent is difficult in slippery conditions and the walker should take *great care* – a stick will aid your progress. Beyond the gate, the walk continues between tall hedges along a path, which after 500 metres joins a track that proceeds to a fingerpost at a minor road on a bend. The route continues straight ahead, along the road, which curves to the right after 100 metres and passes through the village of East Woodhay, back to the Axe and Compasses. Along the way it passes The Old Rectory on the left-hand side, a splendid four-bay country house with a triangular pediment at its northern end. This is the home of Peter Baring of Barings Bank, which was bankrupted by the activities of futures trader Nick Leeson. The nearby red-brick church of St Martin is the parish church of East Woodhay. On the final leg back to East End the road passes Stargrove, a Gothic building with a battlemented French-style roof that lies back to the right.

WW The Wayfarer's Walk – Upper Eastwick Copse to Watership Down (8½ miles)

This leg of the walk keeps to the North Hants Ridgeway, or the Inkpen Ridgeway as it is also called. It passes by Pilot Hill, which is climbed from Faccombe in Pub Walk 3, and continues above Ashmansworth, heading towards the A343, with views of Highclere Castle, 2 miles to the north. The present building is the work of Sir Charles Barry, the designer of the Palace of Westminster, who in the 1840s 'clad' an existing 18th-century mansion with the present Victorian Gothic exterior for the 3rd Earl of Carnarvon. It was the 5th Earl who financed Howard Carter in his amazing discoveries of the tomb of Tutankhamun in Egypt. The route continues past Sidown Hill and round the foot of Beacon Hill to the north. It was on the latter, first discovered by many people as they scramble up from a car park beside the A34, that Sir Geoffrey de Havilland made his epic flights. Just before crossing over the A34, the route passes a stone that commemorates the event; to the north is a dramatic collection of seven barrows.

All along this ridgeway is evidence of the activities of prehistoric man. There are hillforts on both Beacon Hill and Ladle Hill, which is the next major landmark on the route. Built by Iron Age people at about the same time, the two forts defended the major route that passed up from the south, a sort of predecessor to the present A34! The fort on Ladle Hill was, in fact, never finished and therefore shows some details of the methods of construction. Great chalk blocks were used to face the defensive ditches, to prevent loose soil from falling back into them. Beyond Ladle Hill the route of the Wayfarer's Walk passes across the top of Watership Down.

[3] Faccombe
The Jack Russell Inn

The Jack Russell was originally called the George and Dragon and has probably been a pub since the late 1800s. It has always been a freehouse owned by the Faccombe Estates. In 1982, a few years after the estate changed hands, the pub reopened under its new name after a year of building work. Only the part at the back is original; the rest had been built on cinders and needed to be completely rebuilt! The Jack Russell is in the centre of one of the prettiest villages in Hampshire. Opposite is a small pond, which has recently been landscaped and provided with benches. Walkers are welcome to sit here and eat their sandwiches with a drink bought in the pub.

Bar meals are served, with the emphasis on traditional English fare. This is the place to tuck into a steak and kidney pudding in comfortable and attractive surroundings. Leading off the bar is a large conservatory-style restaurant, where game of all sorts is a specialty and the prices are extremely reasonable. This popular freehouse has a beer garden and children's play area and ample car parking. And if you are looking for somewhere to stay the night, the inn has several rooms. Dogs are not allowed inside.

Beers include Theakston Best Bitter, Hampshire Brewery Ironside and Mansfield Old Baily. There is a draught cider and a good selection of wines.

The opening times are from 12 noon to 3 pm and 7 pm to 11 pm (with a restaurant extension to midnight) on weekdays and Saturday, and 12 noon to 10.30 pm on Sundays.

Telephone: 01264 737315.

How to get there: Faccombe is situated midway between Newbury and Andover, to the west of the A343. From the north, it is reached by turning right off the A343, 3 miles south of Highclere, signed to Ashmansworth, which is 2 miles from Faccombe. From the south, the prettiest approach is from Hurstbourne Tarrant, turning off the A343 at the northern edge of the village for a 4-mile run to Faccombe.

Parking: There is ample parking in front of the Jack Russell.

Length of the walk: 6 miles (with a shorter version of 3 miles indicated). Map: OS Landranger 174 Newbury and Wantage (inn GR 391579).

From the estate village of Faccombe this walk climbs up to the North Hampshire Ridgeway, with spectacular views, and then descends to Ashmansworth. It is a walk of wide open countryside, with secretive copses and evidence everywhere of careful husbandry.

The Walk

Leave the Jack Russell and turn left, passing the village bus shelter on the right, donated in 1965 by Miss Alice Roberts. Almost immediately, turn left again and take the road towards the church, signed to West Woodhay. The road passes through the village, past the offices of Faccombe Estates on the left and just before the last house on the right a footpath turns off to the right at a fingerpost. It runs along a track which soon divides into three: our route follows the central track, which descends alongside a hollow way on the right. The track crosses another track after a few hundred metres and then climbs steeply up Pilot Hill, alongside large beeches with massive tangled roots. In certain lighting conditions the down

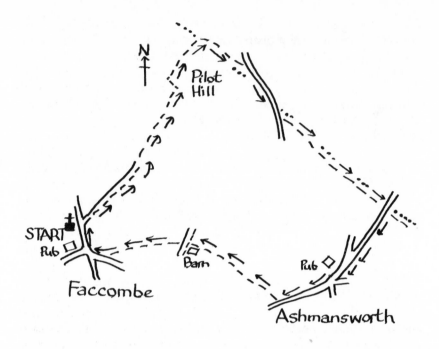

ahead to the right shows traces of ancient fields. The area seethes with pheasants. To the left can be seen the communications mast on Combe Hill in Berkshire, about a mile away.

The track passes through double field gates, along a recent official diversion and continues straight ahead via a stile. The path rises sharply, with a private track turning off to the right, after which it turns sharp left along a field boundary for about 50 metres and then right at a fingerpost by an oak tree. It continues half-right across a field (045° magnetic) to meet the Wayfarer's Walk on the ridge, where you can savour the wonderful views north. (Those wanting a short walk should retrace their steps from here.) Turn **WW** right along the Wayfarer's Walk, which after 500 metres meets a minor road. It follows the road for another 500 metres before slipping off left at a fingerpost, into woodland. The turning is just after the road passes, on the left, the isolated chimney stack and hearth of what was once, perhaps, a shepherd's house. After a kilometre the path meets a minor road; our route turns right, whilst the Wayfarer's Walk continues straight ahead.

The road passes through Ashmansworth, past a road signed to

East Woodhay that comes in from the right near a telephone box. It continues past a former chapel of 1888 and the Plough Inn, where those seeking additional refreshment may care to stop. The route meets the village green, where a road turns right, back to Faccombe. About 500 metres along the road a footpath turns off to the right at a fingerpost and stile on an S-bend. It crosses a crop field, making for the left-hand side of a patch of woodland (300° magnetic) and then falls steeply, before rising to meet a track at a T-junction alongside another wood. The footpath continues ahead and slightly to the left at a fingerpost, through the wood, and proceeds due north, via a recent official diversion along a grassy path between crops. It then runs ahead along the edge of woodland and turns sharp left. Soon, on the left, you will see a dry valley running off in the distance.

The path now passes diagonally through a young coniferous plantation to the right and enters a mainly beech and oak coppice. At the bottom of the coppice the route turns left on a farm track that descends to Curzon Street Farm. The path passes an attractive brick and flint barn on the left and then continues up a steep rise ahead. In the distance to the right can be seen Pilot Hill. The path emerges in woodland and continues to the left, past a clump of laurel, to meet a track, where it turns left. It reaches a minor road, where it turns right to a T-junction, then right again and so back to the Jack Russell.

[4] Ecchinswell
The Royal Oak

The garden of the Royal Oak backs onto a delightful stream that runs through the village. It is a tributary of the river Enborne and is locally called the Ecch (said 'Etch'). The pub is said to date from the 15th century, and, like many old houses, it is, of course, haunted – though none of the bar staff have seen the ghost in question! There is a snug beamed public bar, a games room and a large lounge bar. A varied menu includes vegetarian and fish dishes, pies and rolls.

The opening times are from 12 noon to 3 pm and 5 pm to 11 pm Monday to Friday, 11 am to 11 pm on Saturday and 12 noon to 3 pm and 7 pm to 10.30 pm on Sunday. Meals are served from 12 noon to 2.30 pm and from 7 pm to 9.30 pm on weekdays and Sundays, and all day on Saturday.

Dogs are allowed in the public bar only. Flowers IPA and Original real ales are served, together with Flowers keg and Labatts Blue and Session. Draught cider and a limited number of wines are also on offer.

Telephone: 01635 298280.

How to get there: Ecchinswell lies 5 miles south of Newbury and 3 miles south of the A339 Newbury to Kingsclere road. The Royal Oak is in the main street.

Parking: There is ample car parking at the front and along the side of the pub.

Length of the walk: 6 miles (with a shorter option of 4 miles). Map: OS Landranger 174 Newbury and Wantage and surrounding area (inn GR 499596).

A walk that will be familiar to readers of 'Watership Down'. It curls round Nuthanger Farm and then ascends the North Hants Ridgeway to the west of Watership Down. It descends back to the plain and then skirts the edge of the delightful grounds of Sydmonton Court, returning to the village via farm tracks.

The Walk

Turn right along the road in front of the Royal Oak, passing a right turning signposted Kingclere. After about 200 metres turn right at a fingerpost into a cul-de-sac, past a Victorian school house with a wonderful bell turret. At the foot of the road the footpath continues ahead and then curls round to the left, around a garden. It crosses two stiles and then turns right with a field boundary on the right to another stile and continues straight ahead to meet a minor road. Turn left onto the road and almost immediately turn right along a lovely drove road that runs between hedges. On the left, 2 miles away, can be seen a prominent television mast on Cottington's Hill.

The track soon becomes a footpath running between trees and continues along the left-hand edge of a wood, which follows the line of a hollow way, now blocked with fallen trees. The route then curves round to the right and follows a field boundary, with views of Watership Down to the left, and Ladle Hill and Beacon Hill ahead, eventually meeting a track leading to Nuthanger Farm. Your route turns left along the track and after 500 metres meets a minor road, where you turn right along the road, then after several hundred metres turn left at a crossroads, signed to Ashley Warren. The road climbs steadily up to Nuthanger Down for almost a kilometre in a deep cutting, with stands of beech on either side.

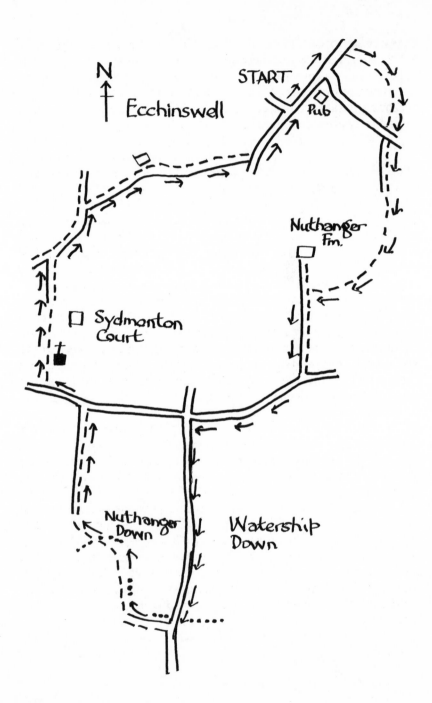

N

Ecchinswell

START

Pub

Nuthanger Fm.

Sydmonton Court

Nuthanger Down

Watership Down

WW From the top of the rise, where the route meets the Wayfarer's Walk, there are magnificent views.

Turn right along the ridge and after 300 metres, beside an electricity pylon, turn right at a stile. A wonderful hollow path, overhung with beech trees, curves down the slope down to reach another stile, beside a metal gate and a horse trough. This must be one of the oldest paths in the area, at least a thousand years old, I would guess. The route continues over the stile on a track that leads towards Sydmonton Court. It meets a minor road, turns left at a stile onto the road and then after 300 metres turns right, and proceeds past the offices of the Sydmonton Court Estate. (Note: A diversion which would take this path up the west side of the estate is under consideration.) To the right is Sydmonton church and further on, on the right, Sydmonton Court, home of the composer Sir Andrew Lloyd Webber. The path continues north, along the drive to the house, and is met at the entrance by a path from the left. Here the route turns right along a track, which soon curls to the left. About 200 metres after the bend, turn off to the right along a track, which passes through a farmyard (currently being developed for housing) to meet a minor road. Turning left leads back to the Royal Oak. For part of the way, the road follows a stream, the Ecch, which further on runs round the bottom of the garden of the pub, on its way to the river Enborne.

WW The Wayfarer's Walk – Watership Down to For Down (3 miles)

Beyond Watership Down, made famous by the book of that title by Richard Adams, the walk passes to the south of Kingsclere, via Cannon Heath Down and Cottington's Hill, where King John once had a hunting lodge. Superb views continue to be a feature of the walk, which passes by White Hill, a notable beauty spot. The area is also noted for its well-drained turf, that is so well suited to training horses. The stables around Kingsclere are famous in racing circles and have produced many winners. Cottington's Hill contains yet another hillfort and also a tall television mast. Hereafter, the Wayfarer's Walk turns south and crosses For Down on its way to Emsworth.

[5] Hannington
The Vine Inn

In common with many pubs, the past history of the Vine is patchy. Some say it was a hunting lodge of the Duke of Wellington. It certainly was for many years a venue for the Vyne and Craven Hunt (note the subtle change in spelling!), until hunt protesters became a problem. At one time it also served as the village store, though from the turn of the century it had become a pub, even a drinking house. Some say it was once called the Shepherd's Crook, which would make sense in this part of the country. Today, it is a thoroughly modern pub belonging to Gales, but still maintains strong links with the village. Leading off from the main bar/lounge is a dining room and a large 'no-smoking' conservatory. Drinks for sale include Gales ales and the very large range of country wines produced by the same company. Bar billiards and darts are available in a side alcove. It has a Children's Certificate, but children under 8 are not allowed in the dining room.

The menu is traditional English fare, with a large variety of pies. Dogs are welcome in the garden only. On a clear day it is said that you can see the Isle of Wight and three counties: Hampshire,

Berkshire and .. Wiltshire? Surrey? .. the landlady was not sure! Answers on a postcard.

The opening times are from 11 am to 2.30 pm and 6 pm to 11 pm on weekdays and Saturday and 12 noon to 3 pm and 7 pm to 10.30 pm on Sundays. Meals are served from 12 noon to 2 pm and from 6.30 pm to 9.30 pm.

Telephone: 01635 298525.

How to get there: Approaching from the north, follow the A339 from Newbury to Kingsclere and 2 miles further south turn right along a minor road, signposted to Hannington, which is 2 miles south-west. The same access road off the A339 can be reached from the south from the Basingstoke ring road.

Parking: There is a large car park alongside the pub.

Length of the walk: 4 miles. Map: OS Landranger 174 Newbury and Wantage (inn GR 540553).

Things ancient and modern dominate this walk, which passes close to the television mast on Cottington's Hill and is crossed by the Portway, the Roman road linking Silchester to Salisbury. The walk climbs to the North Hampshire Ridgeway, falls to the edge of Kingsclere and then ascends the ridge once more to reach Hannington.

The Walk

The road outside the Vine runs to the right into the village centre, with its charming green and memorial 'lychgate' (for one of Queen Victoria's jubilees). Walk down the right-hand side of the churchyard, where a footpath starts beside a large barn. It curls round two sides of the barn and then, in a very odd feature, passes over two stiles scarcely 20 metres apart. This arrangement is presumably to keep the path out of the adjacent farm track. After another 20 metres it passes through a gate and continues ahead on a grassy track, falling slowly in a direction just south of west. The route soon climbs up to For Down, where the well marked path continues half-right, across open downland, with power lines on the right, towards a farm (Walkeridge Farm). On the left before the farm are two former quarries, now scattered with discarded farm

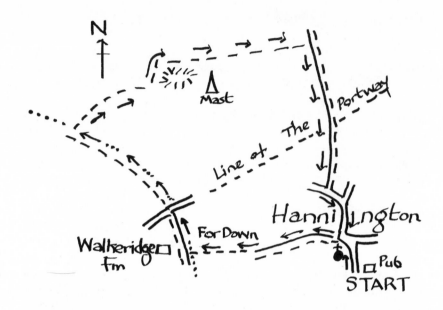

machinery and riddled with rabbit burrows. At the farm, whose name adorns the vane of a wind-pump, the route turns right at a four-way fingerpost, onto a bridleway which after 500 metres dog-legs across a minor road.

WW You are now on the Wayfarer's Walk. The route continues along a grassy path with a field boundary to the left and a thick hedge on the right for about a kilometre. It passes through a two-pole stile to the left of a field gate (belonging to Sydmonton Farms Ltd) and then heads downhill, hugging the field boundary and giving splendid views. The route passes through a field gate and turns right over a large stile. The path turns sharp right again after 20 metres and curls away to the right, reaching two stiles beside earthworks after 600 metres. It continues ahead for 400 metres, with a mature hedge to the right, to a modern three-way fingerpost, where it descends to the left across a field. After 300 metres the route reaches a three-way fingerpost beside an electricity supply line and here it turns right. To the right is a field boundary and to the left a scrubby hanger that looks out to Park House Stables and Kingsclere.

The trail continues to the right via stiles for more than a kilometre, alongside horse jumps (beware passing hooves!), and well past the television mast on Cottington's Hill on the right. Beyond the hanger, the path descends to a stile, where it meets a chalky, rutted bridleway. The route turns right here and continues back to Hannington. After 600 metres it crosses the route of the ancient Portway. At a prominent farm tank on the right, alongside a private farm drive, the route continues ahead (not to the right). The bridleway passes a wood on the right and winds under a high-voltage supply line to meet a minor road at a fingerpost. Turn left onto the road, which soon meets a road from Wolverton at a T-junction. Here, turn right, continue past the former school house and the old post office, and so back to the Vine.

WW The Wayfarer's Walk – For Down to Deane (5 miles)

From For Down, near Hannington, the Wayfarer's Walk circles round in a great loop that keeps several miles away from the new town of Basingstoke to the east. For Down is just south of the Portway, an ancient road that crosses the route of the Wayfarer's Walk just north of Walkeridge Farm. A remarkable stretch of the road to the south-west of the farm is marked by a thin copse, more than 2 miles long, called Caesar's Belt. The route of the Wayfarer's Walk passes through the hamlet of North Oakley and makes towards its larger cousin East Oakley, turning south-west just south of Great Deane Wood, to pass through the delightful village of Deane.

[6] Deane
The Deane Gate Inn

Don't be alarmed if a great wolfhound greets you when you come into this Ushers pub. Mulligan is the landlord's canine bar-hand (not to be confused with Milligan's Mist, a new smooth bitter on offer). Deane Gate was the name of the tollhouse on the London turnpike that once occupied the building, which is thought to be 300 years old. It would certainly have been known to Jane Austen, who was brought up in Steventon nearby, though the rector's daughter would never, of course, have entered its portals. Then the nooks and crannies of this traditional pub, with its horse brasses and oak beams, would have been occupied by less salubrious members of the locality.

A wide range of home-cooked traditional meals and vegetarian dishes is available. There is a garden and dogs on a lead are welcome in the bar – provided Mulligan agrees! Eating one's own food in the garden is not allowed. Amongst the traditional beers on offer are Courage Best, Ushers Best and Founders and a range of brewery seasonal ales, including Summer Madness. There is a good selection of wines and draught cider.

The pub is open from 11 am to 11 pm Monday to Saturday and 12 noon to 10.30 pm on Sundays. Main meals are served from 12 noon to 2.30 pm and 7 pm to 10 pm (9.30 pm on Sunday). Light snacks are available throughout the day.
Telephone: 01256 780226.

How to get there: The Deane Gate Inn is on the B3400, 5 miles west of Basingstoke.

Parking: The Deane Gate Inn has a large main car park and an overflow, which walkers are requested to use for longer-term parking.

Length of the walk: 5½ miles, with a shorter walk of 3 miles indicated. Map: OS Landranger 185 Winchester and Basingstoke (inn GR 547499).

Although close to the new town of Basingstoke, this walk passes through some of the most pleasant country in Hampshire. Just a mile to the west is the source of the river Test, the world famous trout stream that runs to the sea at Southampton.

The Walk

WW Take the road that leads south from the Deane Gate Inn towards Steventon. Outside the pub stands a Wayfarer's Walk sign, 'Inkpen Beacon 18, Emsworth 52'. After 300 metres turn left at Cheesedown Cottage onto a byway, which passes a lovely brick and clinker extension, aptly called Wayfarer's Barn. After about 800 metres the route reaches a crossroads marked with fingerposts and turns left, where it leaves the Wayfarer's Walk. It follows a field boundary, parallel with the Winchester to Basingstoke railway to the right, with Hilsea Cottage in the distance to the left. The path continues over a stile with a fingerpost, along a grassy path between fields, then in about 400 metres, at another fingerpost, the route turns left, with Oakley church visible ahead.

The path continues diagonally through a field and after about 30 metres it forks; you take the left-hand branch, with the church immediately ahead. To the left stand weird fire-ravaged trees, presumably the result of lightning strikes. After 400 metres the path crosses a stile and continues towards the church, where you will find another stile that leads to a fingerpost at the south-west corner

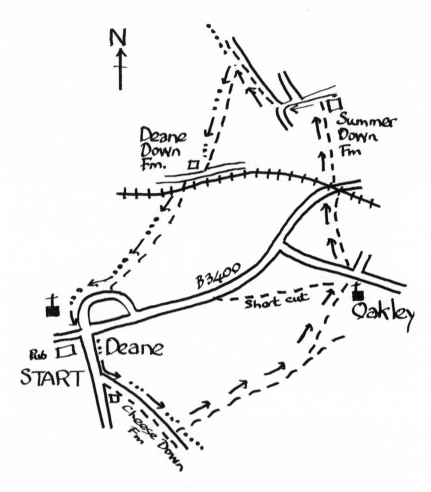

of the old churchyard. (To shorten the walk, turn sharp left just before the church, taking a footpath that runs in a westerly direction to meet the B3400.) The main path passes through an iron kissing-gate near traces of what looks like a ha-ha, with the new burial ground (dating from 1992) on the left. The path emerges in front of the church and continues through a wooden kissing-gate diagonally opposite, on the left-hand corner of Station Road. The path leaves the kissing-gate and crosses to a stile, with several estate cottages down to the right. It reaches another stile, where it forks; you take the right-hand path and cross a field towards a railway arch. To the left of the arch is Clerken Green and a parking area for buses and coaches. The path passes through a galvanised iron kissing-gate and crosses the B3400 (*beware, fast traffic*).

The footpath opposite runs to the right, alongside the chain-link fence of a treatment works. It curves round the fence and continues ahead, along the right-hand edge of a field, towards a three-bay farmhouse (Summer Down Farm). At the farm it turns left (a tempting stile at this point leads in fact into the garden of the farmhouse) and curls round the edge of the farmhouse garden to a fingerpost at a minor road. The route now turns left onto the road, passes a road coming in from Malshanger and Hannington on the right and, further on, where the minor road takes a sharp turn to the left, a footpath runs straight ahead. Almost immediately it turns right at a fingerpost, with an avenue of oaks on the right. You are now on the Wayfarer's Walk.

WW After 500 metres, beside a Wayfarer's Walk signpost, a footpath turns off to the left and cuts back obliquely across a field towards a copse. It crosses a farm track and continues half-left beside a fence to the left. After 50 metres it turns right through a narrow strip of copse, over a stile and then half-left towards the left-hand corner of a farmyard (Deane Down Farm). A stile takes it onto a minor road, where you turn right, passsing the farm and a duckpond. After 100 metres you turn left and cross a brick bridge over the Basingstoke to Andover branch line railway. The footpath continues half-right under three successive electricity supply lines and across two fields towards a cluster of buildings. At the far side of the field the path passes through a hedge behind a corrugated iron barn and along a field boundary to the right. It then proceeds down a driveway to a minor road, where it turns right, to pass through the village of Deane, with its many thatched cottages and All Saints church, back to the B3400 and the pub.

WW The Wayfarer's Walk – Deane to Dummer (4 miles)

This part of the Wayfarer's Walk cuts across the main routes to Winchester and Southampton, notably the main London to Southampton railway just south of Deane and the A30/M3 just before reaching Dummer. It is set for its route down the Candover valley and across the hills towards Emsworth at the head of Chichester Harbour. Just after crossing the railway it reaches Bull's Bushes Copse, formerly owned by the Forestry Commission.

[7] Dummer
The Queen Inn

Whenever the Duchess of York hits the headlines the bar at the Queen Inn fills up with journalists in search of stories. This is because Major Ron Ferguson, the duchess's father, lives nearby at Dummer Down Farm and 'Fergie' herself was brought up locally. No one recalls having seen her in the bar, but before her marriage to Prince Andrew who would have noticed? Certainly the picture of the royal personage on the pub's sign is not her; but no one is sure who it is either. Is it Anne Boleyn or Jane Seymour? Perhaps the original landlord, who is thought to have lived here from at least 1564, would have known. What exists now is a fine old country pub with the traditional accoutrements of its ilk – oak beams, horse brasses and an inglenook fireplace. There is one large open bar with a restaurant area, serving an à la carte menu that responds to local produce, including Dummer pheasant and venison.

At the back of the pub, which is a Courage house, is a large beer garden. There are two draught ciders and a good selection of wines, together with a large range of beers, including Courage Best and Directors, Fuller's London Pride, Wadworth 6X and John Smith's

Bitter. Dogs are well watered outside.

The opening times are from 11 am to 3.30 pm and 5.30 pm to 11 pm, Monday to Saturday, and 12 noon to 3 pm and 7 pm to 11 pm on Sunday. Food is served from 12 noon to 2.30 pm every lunchtime and 6 pm to 10 pm, Monday to Saturday. On Sunday evening, food is served from 7 pm to 9.30 pm.

Telephone: 01256 397367.

How to get there: Dummer is easily reached from junction 7 of the M3, or alternatively by turning west off the B3046 Candover valley road at Axford, between Basingstoke and Alresford.

Parking: There is ample parking at the pub and on the road nearby.

Length of the walk: 2 miles. Map: OS Landranger 185 Winchester and Basingstoke (inn GR 587463).

A short walk around the outskirts of this pretty village, the church of which was a favourite with John Betjeman.

The Walk

From the Queen Inn turn left past a treadmill-operated well (no longer used!), built in 1879 and renovated in 1993 with grants from the local authority and Dummer Golf Club. The road passes the Chapel House Gallery on the left, housed in a Primitive Methodist chapel of 1863, with Dummer Stores on the right. Opposite Glebe Close on the edge of the village a footpath leads off to the left over a waymarked stile and turns left behind gardens. It passes over another stile to meet a track and then dog-legs left and right to continue behind more gardens. It reaches a stile beside an old quarry and then turns right along a barbed wire fence. Ahead is the unwelcome sight of the M3! After about 200 metres it turns left along a field boundary and reaches a stile behind a house on a minor road. Here the route turns left onto the road and almost immediately right at a T-junction, signposted to Axford.

After 100 metres, on the far side of the crescent called Bible Fields, a path runs off from the left and passes through a kissing-gate at a fingerpost. It is a pretty path that winds through an area that is lightly wooded and low-lying. After emerging from the trees

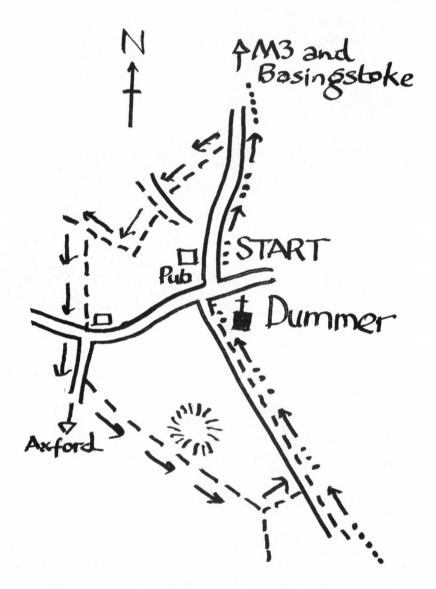

it follows the right-hand side of a field. The path then splits and we take the right-hand limb, past a line of willows that are a vivid rust colour in the winter. They stand on a high bank that hides a low-lying area – presumably a pond at certain times of year. The path

All Saints Church, Dummer.

rises gently with a field boundary to the right. It then splits and you follow the left-hand arm, which runs across a crop field (050° magnetic) to meet a concrete track, which is part of the Wayfarer's **WW** Walk. Turn left and pass through a farmyard, with Dummer House to the left, to meet a minor road at a bus shelter (donated by Mrs Andrew Ferguson in 1952). Turn right and then almost immediately left at the church and so back to the pub.

WW **The Wayfarer's Walk – Dummer to Brown Candover (5 miles)**
The Candover valley, which runs down to Alresford, is a quiet part of the countryside. But the Wayfarer's Walk manages to tread an even quieter route, by means of bridleways and footpaths that take it in a southerly direction. It crosses high lands that are now intensively farmed, though often as remote as the time when they were forest or open downland. The path descends to Brown Candover, an archetypal English village, with cricket in the summer.

[8] Preston Candover
The Purefoy Arms

The Purefoy Arms stands in the centre of the village, opposite the restored village pump. It is the sort of pub where at lunchtimes most of the customers arrive in four-wheel drive vehicles or tractors. Outside work hours it adopts a different style, with live traditional jazz on Thursday evenings and Sunday lunchtimes. The building dates from 1860 and it may always have been a pub. It takes its name from a French admiral who married a local heiress. There are lounge and public bars, with dogs only allowed in the latter. Eating one's own food in the garden is definitely off-limits at this pub. It is an Ushers house and has an extensive wine list.

The opening times are from 11 am to 2.30 pm and and 6 pm to 11 pm Monday to Saturday and 12 noon to 3 pm and 7 pm to 10.30 pm on Sunday. Meals are served from 12 noon to 2 pm and 6.30 pm to 10 pm during the week and 12 noon to 2.30 pm and 7 pm to 9.30 pm on Sunday. You are advised to book.

Telephone: 01256 389258.

How to get there: Preston Candover is strung out along the

B3046 Basingstoke to Alresford road, 5 miles north of Alresford. The Purefoy Arms is in the centre of the village.

Parking: There is parking outside the pub and on the road nearby.

Length of the walk: 6 miles, with a shorter walk of 4 miles. Map: OS Landranger 185 Winchester and Basingstoke (inn GR 606417).

The Candover valley is one of those little-known areas where sheep and farmers have moulded the landscape for centuries. Much of this walk is through remote highlands where the odd tractor and a few pheasants are all you are likely to meet. A resident family of deer can usually be glimpsed hereabouts.

The Walk

Turn left along the B3046 outside the Purefoy Arms and just past the village hall turn left onto a bridleway that makes its way across a field, with tennis courts to the left, to reach an avenue of trees. It then runs gently uphill under a power line in a north-westerly direction. It curves round to the right, with a thick hedge and woodland to the left, eventually meeting a track, with farm buildings ahead, where the route turns right and then almost immediately left onto a farm-track-cum-bridleway that heads in a north-westerly direction along the right-hand side of the farm buildings. The track drops into a hollow and as it climbs up again, ignore a further track which forks off to the left. Our route continues through a patch of lovely mixed woodland scattered with laurel. The track emerges from the woodland and bends to the right, then right again, following the edge of the wood to a country road, with a house (Poasley Farmhouse) to the left.

The route turns left onto the road at a fingerpost and an automated farm gate and then keeps to the road for about a kilometre. After several hundred metres it passes Flockmore Cottage on the right, a Victorian brick and flint house with outbuildings and what appears to be a cricket pavilion. Further on, on a slight right-hand bend in the road, a footpath signed with a fingerpost turns off to the left. This provides a short cut back to Preston Candover for those who want a shorter walk. The full route continues on the road to meet the Wayfarer's Walk, at a point

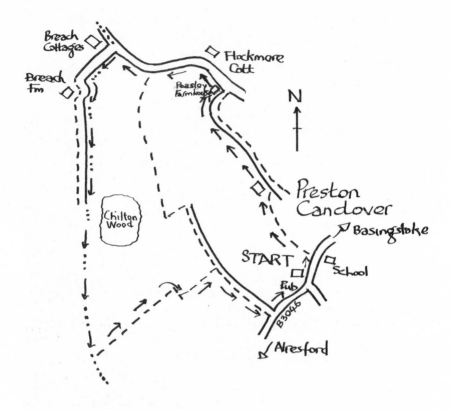

where a small cul-de-sac turns off to Breach Farm to the left, by a fingerpost, opposite a farm gate and alongside a white house. The **WW** side road soon reaches a triple fingerpost, with the Wayfarer's Walk continuing ahead. Your route turns left, through the farmyard on a track that soon dog-legs right and left and continues in a southerly direction for about 2 kilometres, disregarding several side-paths.

After about a kilometre the track ascends and becomes grassier, with Chilton Wood to the left. It then follows the right-hand edge of a lovely strip of woodland, with huge oaks and beeches, emerging to meet a track that turns off left, just before a young plantation on the left. It proceeds in a north-easterly direction for about a kilometre and then turns sharp right. After 40 metres you will reach an easily missed stile, buried in the hedge to the left. Cross the stile and continue straight ahead for a few hundred

The old village pump at Preston Candover.

metres, with a hedge on the left, to a well hidden fingerpost on the left. Turn right onto a track (also on the route of the short cut referred to above) that soon descends to meet a tarmac road that passes houses to meet the B3046. Just before the road, on the right, is the chancel and graveyard of the old church of Preston Candover. Turn left along the road to return to the Purefoy Arms.

[9] Totford
The Woolpack

The Woolpack is thought to have earned its name from the proximity of the Ox-Drove (used for everything except oxen), an ancient road used for driving sheep and cattle. The pub was a staging post for the drovers, who generally went on to Farnham. It stands near the diminutive stream that now occupies the Candover valley and, so it is said, was once able to take small boats to the Itchen and so to the sea. Perhaps in a pub the story is what counts! This certainly is the case with the Woolpack ghost, a lady with long hair, who uses the bar intercom and plays the fruit machines. One day the familiar sounds of the jackpot alarmed the landlord in what he thought was a deserted pub. He rushed to collect the winnings, but they had disappeared! The listed building dates from the 16/17th century and has a fine flagstone floor that is said to have come from a Roman building at Abbotstone. Some say that the pub was originally in the cottage down by the stream, but flooding was a problem.

The changing selection of real ale includes classics such as Gales HSB, Palmers IPA, Eldridge Pope Hardy Country Ale and

Cheriton Pots Ale. The mainly French wine list is also extensive.

There is one large comfortable open bar (dogs welcome) and an adjoining restaurant. The food is a mix of traditional English fare and those classic continental dishes that have almost become 'English'. A large garden with chickens and ducks is alongside the pub. Walkers are welcome to eat their food in the garden, but ought to play fair with mine host. There are 10 bedrooms.

The pub is open from 11.30 am to 3 pm and 6 pm to 11 pm Monday to Saturday and 12 noon to 3 pm and 7 pm to 10.30 pm on Sundays. Food is available from 12 noon to 2 pm and 7 pm to 10 pm.

Telephone: 01962 732101.

How to get there: Totford is a small hamlet situated 3 miles north of Old Alresford, on the B3046 Alresford to Basingstoke road.

Parking: The Woolpack has a good sized car park.

Length of the walk: 4 miles. Map: OS Landranger 185 Winchester and Basingstoke (inn GR 571379).

As its name suggests, the Ox-Drove, part of which is included in this walk, is an old drove road, along which animals were driven to market before the advent of lorries. This walk explores the Candover valley, via the charming village of Brown Candover, and runs for some way along the first waters of the Candover Stream, which is the heart and soul of this lovely valley. Water underfoot is good news in these parts.

The Walk

WW The track on the south side of the Woolpack is on the Wayfarer's Walk. Walk in an easterly direction on a broad chalky path between hedges, which dog-legs and soon gives fine views across the Candover valley. It shortly reaches farm buildings and a concrete road; here we leave the Wayfarer's Walk, which turns off to the right. On reaching a T-junction on the Ox-Drove, with a barn on the left, turn right, then after 50 metres the track curves round to the left and continues in a north-easterly direction. After a few hundred metres, leave the Ox-Drove by turning left on a path that runs beside a narrow strip of woodland. Soon, the path bears

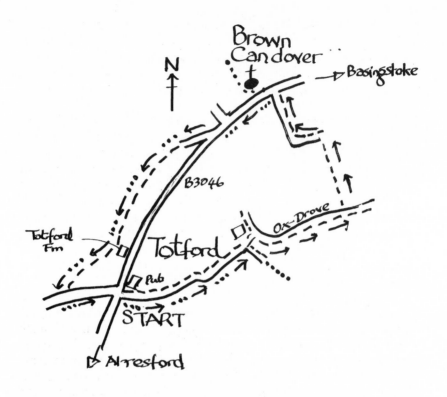

left, with Brown Candover church visible ahead. After a similar distance it turns right, passing through a cluster of farm buildings before meeting the B3046 Candover valley road.

Brown Candover is all that the rural idyll requires, for it boasts a pretty church (with a wonderful organ), a cricket green and a pavilion with a clock. Linger awhile if you wish, though the route turns left along the road. It continues past an imposing gateway with iron gates on the left, alongside the boundary wall of Manor Farm on the right, and then passes a minor road, signposted to Woodmancott. Remain on the main road, pass a pond on the left, then where the road bends to the left, we keep straight on into a cul-de-sac, at a Wayfarer's Walk sign. There are extensive wetlands on the left. Soon the road bends round to the right, petering out in a track, whilst our route continues ahead along a bridleway, still following the Wayfarer's Walk. To the left can be seen the source of the Candover Stream. Ahead lies Totford Farm, with its black-roofed barns. The path passes to the right of the farm, whilst the stream moves away from the path to pass in front of the farm, and, beyond, the Woolpack can be glimpsed to the left. The route continues on the path to meet a minor road, where we turn left and cross over the Candover Stream, and so back to the pub.

WW **The Wayfarer's Walk – Brown Candover to Alresford (7 miles)**
Totford is within this leg of the walk, which winds down the valley of the Candover Stream. This diminutive waterway was once much larger and still nourishes a string of villages (and the lake of Northington Grange), before running into the river Itchen just west of Alresford. The route from Brown Candover follows a footpath to Totford and then turns east for a while to follow the Ox-Drove, an ancient road used for driving sheep and cattle. It was part of a system of drove roads, including the Lunway and the Harrow Way, and enabled animals to be driven from the West Country into Surrey and Kent.

The Wayfarer's Walk goes over Abbotstone Down, which takes its name from the 'lost village' of Abbotstone. About 32 acres of the down is now a Country Park owned by Hampshire County Council and has become a popular spot for recreation. The route here passes Oliver's Battery, an Iron Age hillfort that takes its name from Oliver Cromwell, although it does not seem to have been used during the Civil War. The walk continues to Abbotstone itself, which was once a somewhat larger settlement, as indicated by the humps and bumps of former houses and other records. The Wayfarer's Walk continues across to Itchen Stoke Down, on the flanks of the Itchen valley, before turning east to Alresford, or to be precise New Alresford, which was 'new' in the 13th century, when it was founded by the Bishop of Winchester.

[10] New Alresford
The Globe on the Lake

A wonderfully positioned pub on the edge of Alresford Pond, with its reed beds and wealth of birdlife. It is said to have been a pub since at least 1700, when it was rebuilt. The pond was originally built to keep freshwater fish at a time when the Bishop of Winchester founded New Alresford in the 13th century. In the summer the garden of the Globe is a splendid spot for alfresco supping and may be very busy. Inside, there is a dining room and a large, beamed L-shaped bar with open fires.

This is a Courage pub owned by a landlord–chef team, which means imaginative home-cooked food using fresh local produce – definitely not ordinary pub grub. There are two menus, one for the bar and garden and another for the restaurant, where you can eat in style. Amongst the beers served, all real ales, are John Smith's, Courage Best, Wadworth 6X and Marston's Pedigree. There is also draught cider and a good selection of wines.

The opening times are from 11 am to 3 pm and 6 pm to 10.30 pm Monday to Saturday and 12 noon to 3 pm and 7 pm to 10.30 pm on Sunday. Meals are served from 12 noon to 2 pm and 6 pm (7 pm on

Sunday) to 9.30 pm, though the restaurant is not open on Sunday and Monday evenings.

Telephone: 01962 732294.

How to get there: New and Old Alresford are really one large village, which is located 7 miles east of Winchester. From the B3047, which passes through the village, turn northwards down Broad Street in the centre. The Globe will be found on the right, beyond a dog-leg bend at the foot of Broad Street.

Parking: Park in Broad Street, or in the pay and display car park by the Mid-Hants Railway (Watercress Line).

Length of the walk: 3 miles, with a shorter option of 2 miles. Map: OS Landranger 185 Winchester and Basingstoke (inn GR 589330).

'Water, water everywhere' could well be the motto for this walk, which follows the river Alre and passes some of the many ponds it feeds. New Alresford was chosen in the 13th century by the Bishop of Winchester as a suitable place to found a new town, for its waters were ideal for powering mills. Today, it is noted for its watercress.

The Walk

From the Globe, walk back towards the village centre via The Soke (a name which means the bishop's lands), with the Old Fire Station **WW** of 1881 on the left. The Wayfarer's Walk is met at the foot of Broad Street, where you turn right and right again, down Mill Lane. Almost immediately, turn left into Ladywell Lane on a path which passes Ladywell Cottage, with its attractive white wicket fence, and then passes between a stream on the right and Ladywell Lakes, situated behind a fence on the left. It passes a small public garden on the left, given in 1951 in memory of 'the fallen in the two great wars' to the people of Alresford by the Rt Hon Sir Francis Lindley of the Weir House, Alresford. Walk by the Fulling Mill, a fine timbered house dating from the 13th century, and continue past rushing water to the foot of a cul-de-sac, where you turn right at a fingerpost. The path then follows the stream on the right, skirting a recreation field on the left, then passing another lake on the left, edged by that rare sight, a laid hedge.

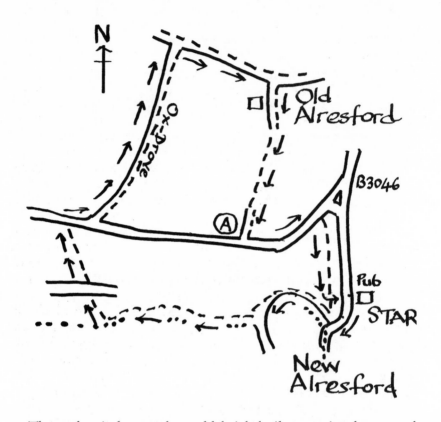

The path winds round an old brick-built pumping house and dog-legs across to the other side of the stream to rise to houses. It proceeds past the houses under huge horse chestnut trees and, soon after passing a private track on the right, turns sharp right up a flight of steps cut in a bank and continues across a field up to a minor road. Here it dog-legs left and right to a fingerpost, then continues through a field gate and heads up the right-hand side of a field, alongside a hedge, where the farmer has thoughtfully left a good wide path. Behind are views of Arlebury House, once visited by Charles Kingsley, author of *The Water Babies*, and its lakes, whilst Alresford spreads out to the left. Ahead, to the right, is Old Alresford church and a kilometre to the north lies the site of the deserted village of Abbotstone.

The path emerges on a minor road at a field gate and fingerpost.

Our route turns right and then left along the Ox-Drove, an ancient drovers' lane. (Those requiring a shorter walk can continue along the minor road to Point A below). The Ox-Drove winds its way between hedges and after 800 metres meets another track, where the route turns right onto a deep-cut track, which is another part of the Ox-Drove. This continues to the edge of a farmyard on the right, which has a footpath running through it. You turn right onto this footpath and follow it straight ahead, leaving Manor Farm Barns, including a large thatched barn, on the right. About 100 metres further on the footpath leaves the farm track and cuts up right over a stile to continue beside a hedge. Beyond the hedge are watercress beds, overlooked by Old Alresford church, once served by a clergyman whose wife, Mary Sumner, founded the Mothers' Union at Alresford in the last century.

The path emerges onto a gravel track that leads to a minor road at a fingerpost (Point A). The route turns left, passes over a stream and enters a 30 mph zone. Here a footpath turns off right across running water, passing more watercress beds on the left. Watercress can be bought from a chest beside the path, where there is an honesty box. The path continues past Arle Mill, beyond which can be seen the causeway that holds back the waters of Alresford Pond, originally an episcopal fishpond. The route emerges by the pounding cascades of Town Mill. A path turns left between walls just beyond the mill and crosses a small bridge. It turns sharp right and emerges opposite the Globe, on the drive of Mill Lane House.

▰▰▰ The Wayfarer's Walk – New Alresford to Cheriton (3 miles)

Broad Street, New Alresford, is as elegant a Georgian street as you will see anywhere. It replaced the fabric of the old medieval town after a number of devastating fires. The Wayfarer's Walk leaves the town and passes close to the railway station that once served the Mid-Hants Railway between Alton and Winchester. It was known locally as the Watercress Line on account of the large quantities of that winter salad grown in the area and once taken to market by train. Closed by British Rail in 1973, the line re-opened under the management of private enthusiasts to operate a steam railway, which now runs between Alresford and Alton, where it connects with the services of South Western Trains. Hereafter, there are two alternative routes for the Wayfarer's Walk, namely, one through the pretty village of Tichborne and another to the east,

The old fulling mill at New Alresford.

which rejoins the Tichborne route at Cheriton Mill. Tichborne has been associated with a family of that name since the Norman Conquest. In a celebrated court case of the last century, a Wapping butcher who returned from Australia to claim the inheritance of a long lost son of the family was eventually found to be an imposter and sent to prison. The Tichborne Dole is a custom dating from the 12th century, in which every parishioner receives gratis a quantity of flour on Lady Day. The Wayfarer's Walk continues on to Cheriton, across gentle countryside fed by the headwaters of the river Itchen.

[11] Cheriton
The Flower Pots Inn

Given the opportunity a few years ago to buy the Flower Pots Inn, where he knew the sitting tenant, Paul Tickner went ahead and turned a sleepy pub into a roaring success. He then founded Cheriton Brewhouse on the site, which now supplies the pub (and 30 others) with beers from the barrel, namely, Pots Ale, Cheriton Best and Diggers Gold. They also have plans to make their own cider. Cheriton has never been so well known since the Civil War!

The pub was originally built in 1830 as Flower Pots Farm by a gardener from Northington Grange, though it soon became an alehouse. There are two bars, a carpeted saloon bar on the left and a bar with a tiled floor on the right. The pub has a large beer garden. There is a menu of good honest bar food. The pub has five double bedrooms in a converted stable block. Dogs are welcome in the bar and the landlord is not averse to walkers leaving their car in the car park (but not throughout opening hours), or eating their own sandwiches with a beer in the garden. But it would be a courtesy to ask first.

Opening hours are from 12 noon to 2.30 pm and and 6 pm to 11 pm Monday to Saturday (with later opening on Saturday

afternoons in the summer) and 12 noon to 3 pm and 7 pm to 10.30 pm on Sunday. Meals are served from 12 noon to 2 pm and 7 pm to 9 pm, except on Sunday evenings.
  Telephone: 01962 771318.

How to get there: From the A272 Winchester to Petersfield road turn north into Cheriton along the B3046 and on entering the village turn left up the hill. The Flower Pots Inn will be found a few hundred metres on the left.

Parking: The pub has a large car park.

Length of the walk: 4 miles. Map: OS Landranger 185 Winchester and Basingstoke (inn GR 581283).

Cheriton is one of the prettiest villages in Hampshire. This walk runs over open fields, woodland paths and country roads, and passes the site of the Battle of Cheriton of 1644, which was a notable event in the Civil War. There are extensive downland views.

The Walk

From the Flower Pots Inn turn right and walk down the hill to the junction. Turn left and almost immediately right on a fork to the right of the war memorial, with Cheriton Garage and the post office ahead. Fifty metres beyond the post office, turn right (you are now on the Wayfarer's Walk) across a tiny brick bridge over the river Itchen (Point A) and then sharp right again, in front of the primary school. Ahead is a gravel drive, with a footpath (called Jane Long's Path) turning to the left just before it, to the right of the entrance to Martyrwell. It heads uphill between a wall and a fence and comes out in a field. The route continues ahead to a stile, where it turns right along the edge of a field, with views ahead of New Cheriton. After 100 metres it turns left in the corner of the field and within a similar distance reaches a stile. Proceed ahead along a track between hedges, which after a few hundred metres meets another track at a T-junction (Point B), and parts company with the Wayfarer's Walk. (Alternative route: from the last stile mentioned, turn sharp right and after 20 metres take a footpath on the left, which runs down a field, past a long barrow on the right to a stile in the bottom left-hand corner – though it should be noted

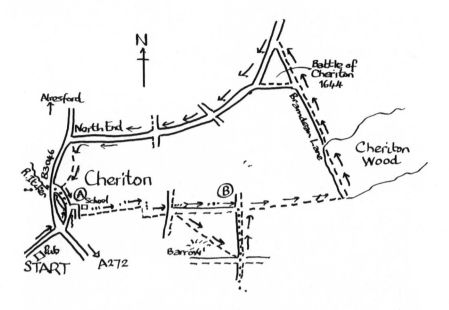

that usage seems to have diverted this path to the right of the barrow, after which it meets a track, where you should turn left to reach the bottom left-hand stile, at a point where another track crosses. Turning left at this stile in a northerly direction leads to Point B above.)

The route continues to the east through a wooden gate on a footpath with a hedge to the right. At the far side of the field it meets Cheriton Wood, where you turn left along an old track (Bramdean Lane) that runs just inside the wood in a north-westerly direction. It emerges from the wood and falls to a dew pond, with distant views of Gander Down to the left. Further on, where a private road comes in from the left, is the site where the Battle of Cheriton was fought in 1644 – though you'd never know it!

The track continues to meet a minor road, where the route turns acutely to the left at a fingerpost. It continues on this road between rabbit-ridden banks to the B3046 at North End, where it turns left in front of an L-shaped thatched cottage (Rose Cottage). It passes by a length of thatched wall – a rare sight these days – crosses a stile and then runs along the rear of gardens, passing an oak tree dramatically planted on the spoils of an old pit. It curves to the right and passes alongside a small, cruckish brick-and-flint cottage with a

The village green, Cheriton.

half-tiled, half-thatched roof. At a stile alongside the dwelling, turn left to Point A and so back to the pub.

WW The Wayfarer's Walk – Cheriton to Wind Farm (4 miles)

From Cheriton the Wayfarer's Walk continues to Hinton Ampner, a tiny village with a grand house with fine gardens, owned since 1986 by the National Trust. There has been a manor house at Hinton Ampner since the middle of the 16th century, though the present house was rebuilt after an earlier one was destroyed by fire in 1960. The walk continues to Kilmeston and on to Wind Farm, across open countryside. Here it meets the South Downs Way and the two long-distance walks continue along the same route for a short distance.

[12] Beauworth
The Milbury's

Since 1984, this freehouse has used the local name for the Mill Barrows, a nearby group of prehistoric burial mounds. It was formerly known as the Fox and Hounds and is said to have been a pub since the late 17th or early 18th centuries. Its main bar is a gem of olde-worlde charm, with a large open log fire and hand-hewn tables. Beyond is the Wheel Room with a 300 ft deep well (yes, 300!), which is believed to date from the 10th or 11th centuries. The great depth was necessary to get down to the water table from the hilltop and it required a treadwheel (the existing one is 250 years old) to wind up the bucket. Customers are sometimes, on request, given lumps of ice to drop down the well – as you wait for the splash, spare a thought for the welldiggers! The pub also has a family area and a skittle alley. There is a traditional bar menu (beef and Guinness pie is a speciality) and a separate restaurant with a table d'hôte menu. Dogs, children and families are all welcome! Eating one's own food in the garden is permitted with a drink bought from the bar. The pub has two rooms available for bed and breakfast.

Real ales include Milburys Bitter, specially brewed for the pub and described as 'fruity and hoppy with malty undertones'. Other featured beers may include Hampshire Brewery King Alfred's and Pendragon. There is also a draught cider, a good selection of wines and Gales country wines.

The opening times are from 11 am to 2.30 pm and 6 pm to 11 pm on weekdays and Saturday, and 12 noon to 3 pm and 6 pm to 10.30 pm on Sunday. The pub is open all day on Saturday and Sunday in the summer. Meals are served from 12 noon to 2 pm and 6 pm to 10 pm.

Telephone: 01962 771248.

How to get there: Milbury's is situated 6 miles east of Winchester and 1 mile south of the A272. It is best reached by turning south off the A272 at the Cheriton junction, signposted to Beauworth. Alternatively, it can be reached by turning west off the A32 Meon valley road at Warnford and continuing along a country road for about 4 miles.

Parking: Milbury's has ample car parking space.

Length of the walk: 4 miles. Map: OS Landranger 185 Winchester and Basingstoke (inn GR 569246).

This walk is in a remote part of Hampshire, where small scattered farming settlements with long histories lie in high rolling downlands. The route goes by field and wood and hill that show the true meaning of the word 'settled'.

The Walk

From Milbury's take a minor road that runs north to Beauworth and Cheriton. During the winter this road is sometimes closed to traffic by flooding, despite the cutting of large flood-relief ditches. After about 100 metres a lane forks off to the left along the route of the South Downs Way (marked by an acorn emblem). Disregard this and head downhill along the road, past Yew Tree Farmhouse (yes, there are yews) and into the delightful hamlet of Beauworth. A cluster of thatched cottages is grouped around the small village green, with the church of St James, which dates from 1838, up to the left. The key is available from Church Cottage, the first cottage

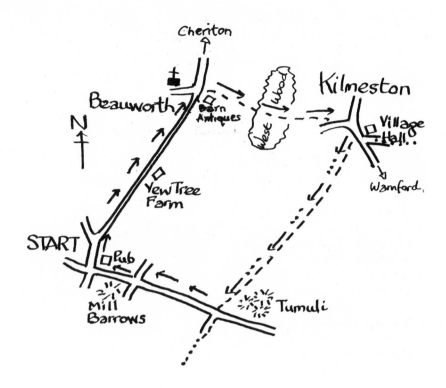

below the church. Your route continues to the right at a stile and fingerpost, just past the green, where a footpath runs along the northern side of the premises occupied by Barn Antiques. The path follows a line of oak trees and after 200 metres passes over a stile hidden in undergrowth on the right. It continues half-left across the corner of a field in a south-easterly direction to another stile. To the right is a large brick water tower.

The footpath runs down the field, leaving a delightfully wild small pond to the right, to reach another stile at the edge of a wood (West Wood). From here the path runs in an easterly direction through the wood, crosses a grassy track and continues itself as a grassy track, soon to meet another track at a T-junction on the eastern edge of the wood. Continue straight ahead, over a stile and between a tall hedge on the left and an open field to the right, eventually reaching a minor road on the edge of Kilmeston at a fingerpost. Here the route turns left, then almost immediately right at a T-junction, signposted to Warnford. A short distance ahead is the village hall, a building of some character. Opposite the hall, follow a fingerpost that points in a southerly direction and join the Wayfarer's Walk.

WW The footpath continues via a series of single and double stiles across four paddocks to a short stretch of tall hedging. The route then passes over a stile through the hedge at a fingerpost and runs half-left across a crop field in a south-westerly direction. The landmark to make for on the horizon is a tall tree alongside a telegraph pole. Here a useful navigation mark, namely, a large yellow disc, marks the position of a double fingerpost and stile. On the other side of the stile the path continues across another crop field, with a farm lying in a hollow ½ mile to the right. The path falls and rises again in a line as straight a Roman road! At the far side is another yellow navigation disc at a stile, with woodland to the right. The route continues half-left through parkland, up a gentle slope alongside a fence. On the skyline to the left can be seen three tumuli.

The path emerges on a minor road at a triple fingerpost, where it meets the South Downs Way coming in from the right. Here you leave the Wayfarer's Walk, which now joins the South Downs Way for a short distance. Your route turns right along the South Downs Way, heading west back to Milbury's. For about 800 metres, until you reach the drive to Preshaw House on the left, opposite a turning to Kilmeston on the right, the path follows a bridleway separated from the road by a hedge. On the left, just past the drive, can be seen the Mill Barrows which have given the pub its name, though the apostrophe in The Milbury's is idiosyncratic.

WW The Wayfarer's Walk – Wind Farm to the Meon valley (6 miles)
Wind Farm is less than a mile to the east of the Milbury's. Hereafter, the Wayfarer's Walk continues 'hand in hand' with the South Downs Way as far as Lomer Farm, which takes its name from a village that disappeared at the end of the 14th century. The route continues to Betty Mundy's Bottom, a local name with a *double entendre*, for the lady in question was said to have been a sort of courtesan-robber who lured travellers to their death. Hmm! The Wayfarer's Walk descends into the valley of the river Meon. There are pub walks centred on Meonstoke, Soberton and Droxford, where the Wayfarer's Walk emerges from its lofty strides.

[13] Meonstoke
The Buck's Head Inn

If you come to the Buck's Head on Boxing Day you may see the Hambledon and Hursley Hunt (and probably the 'huntsabbers'!) assembling for their traditional sport. In the summer you may be lucky and see Morris Men (and women) dancing outside the pub. Events such as these seem quite natural in the setting of the Buck's Head, which is on the edge of the countryside, opposite the river Meon and alongside Meonstoke church. Adjacent to the pub is a large garden – it is as typical as the typical country pub can be. Inside, are public and lounge bars, reached by separate doors, with open log fires and oak beams. All this is expected in a pub that dates from the 16th or 17th centuries, although some even claim the 12th century.

There are several daily specials on the board and all food is fresh and cooked to order. Beers include Morland Old Speckled Hen and Cheriton Pots Ale, whilst draught cider and wines, including Gales country wines, are also available. Clean dogs are welcome in the public bar.

The opening times are 11 am to 3 pm and 6 pm to 11 pm on

weekdays, 11 am to 11 pm on Saturdays and 12 noon to 3 pm and 7 pm to 10.30 pm on Sundays. Meals are available from 12 noon to 2 pm and 7 pm to 9 pm, except Monday evenings.
Telephone: 01489 877313.

How to get there: Meonstoke is located just off the A32 Alton to Fareham road, about 4 miles north-east of Bishop's Waltham. The Buck's Head Inn is 100 metres to the east of the village church, which stands alongside the A32.

Parking: There is a large car park opposite the pub.

Length of the walk: 5 miles. Map: OS Landranger 185 Winchester and Basingstoke (inn GR 612201).

The Meon valley is a secret that locals tend to keep to themselves. This walk climbs up the western flank of the valley and explores some of its ancient woodland before coming 'the back way' into the outskirts of Exton, a village (like most of the Meon's settlements) with a Saxon pedigree.

The Walk

From the Buck's Head, walk back to the A32 and turn left. After about 100 metres take a footpath to the right which crosses a field to a stile on the left of a copse. The path then runs up a steep bank to a gate, to the left of which is a makeshift stile. At the other side of the stile the route continues in a westerly direction, with a thick hedge on the right. It keeps to this hedge, dog-legging right and left around a modern barn, for more than a kilometre, to meet a minor road opposite Corhampton Golf Club (founded in 1891). The route turns left along the road and after a few hundred metres turns **WW** right, just before a crossroads, onto the waymarked Wayfarer's Walk. This winds its way downhill through woodland, keeping the golf course on the right (beware golf balls!). It **never** enters the course. After the 16th tee the course extends to both left and right for a short distance, but the footpath keeps going ahead. At the 7th hole the path curls round to the left and descends steeply to the B3035. The route dog-legs left and right across the road and continues past a farm (Steynes Farm) on a bridleway.

You are still on the Wayfarer's Walk, which soon turns off to the

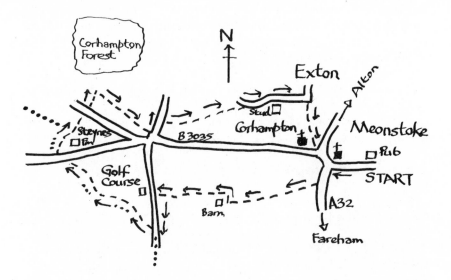

left to curl round Bottom Copse. Your path runs alongside a chain-link fence on the right and then turns right into woods. There are plenty of 'Private' notices to shepherd the errant rambler! The footpath soon turns left and runs in a roughly north-easterly direction to reach a minor road, which it crosses, and continues towards woodland (Corhampton Forest), to meet a track on the edge of the forest. From here, the route strikes back across a crop field in a south-easterly direction to meet the B3035 at a crossroads, where it turns left on a minor road. It leads north and after 200 metres turns right at a fingerpost onto a footpath, with a hedge on the right.

At the far end of the hedge is a brick-built tank, from where the path runs down a crop field in a north-easterly direction (080° magnetic) towards a copse. It enters the left-hand edge of the copse, where there is a yellow marker and a fingerpost. The footpath meets a track which it follows to the right, before striking down to the north-east corner of the copse. (If you meet a high-fenced enclosure on the left, retrace your steps to regain the footpath.) From the copse the path continues through a grassy bottom to a white field gate alongside an apology of a stile. Twenty metres further on the path passes through the hedge and meets a track. Turn right and follow the track past Exton Stud, where it becomes a

Meonstoke church.

road. This soon meets another road coming in from the left, and continues downhill before making a sharp turn to the left. At this point a signed footpath leads off to the right across fields, through two kissing-gates, with the river Meon on the left, to reach Corhampton church. If you wonder at the great height of this building, it is because it is a rare example of a Saxon church. Turning left leads to the A32 and so back to the Buck's Head Inn.

[14] Droxford
The White Horse Inn

There can be few pubs with a 40 ft deep floodlit well in the gents. Apart from this, the White Horse is a traditional coaching inn, offering a full range of facilities, including overnight accommodation in three bedrooms. You may prefer the lounge bar, complete with *The Times* daily, the snug, or the Stable Bar (as the public bar is called). There is also a children's area and a restaurant in this relaxing and comfortable inn, which is reputed to be 400 or 500 years old.

Home-made food is the rule, with specials that include gourmet fish pie and a steak and Guinness pie made with best chuck steak. The fish is also good, with haddock and local trout smoked nearby at Exton. Beers include Wadworth 6X, Exmoor Gold, Hampshire Hog and Hobglobin. Dogs are welcome in the Stable Bar, or on a lead on the patio area at the rear.

The opening times are from 11 am to 3 pm and 6 pm to 11 pm Monday to Saturday and 12 noon to 3 pm (or later) and 7 pm to 10.30 pm on Sunday. Food is served from 12 noon to 2 pm and 7 pm to 9.45 pm.

Telephone: 01489 877490.

How to get there: Droxford is situated about 3 miles east of Bishop's Waltham on the A32 Alton to Fareham road, which forms the main street through the village. The White Horse Inn is just south of the church.

Parking: There is a small car park behind the pub.

Length of the walk: 5½ miles. Map: OS Landranger 185 Winchester and Basingstoke (inn GR 606181).

This walk takes in the river Meon, Old Winchester Hill National Nature Reserve and the deserted cuttings of a disused railway line. It is a challenging route that reaches the heart of the Meon valley.

The Walk

Turn right onto the A32 and right again into the left-hand side of the churchyard. A path curls round behind the church and then turns left to cross the river Meon via two plank bridges. As **WW** indicated by a fingerpost in front of the church, you are now on a leg of the Wayfarer's Walk, which turns off to the right at the second plank bridge, on its way to Soberton. Your route continues straight on, passing a huge horse chestnut tree to reach a kissing-gate, where it turns sharp left and winds through woodland. There are fine views to the left across the valley. The path continues past a fingerpost to the left and emerges just before houses, where it turns onto a drive. Turn left to meet the B2150, then right under a railway arch. Disregard the turning to Soberton on the right and continue on the B2150, with The Hurdles Motel and pub on the right. After about 100 metres a very small single-track road turns off to the left, just after Walton Farm, and climbs steadily towards Old Winchester Hill for more than a kilometre. It passes Watton Farm on the left and continues ahead at a crossroads, signposted to Clanfield and Horndean.

Beyond the crossroads two footpaths turn off to the left. The one you want is the second one, reached after about 300 metres. It crosses a stile and descends in a north-easterly direction for 500 metres. It then rises to a field gate and crosses a minor road to meet a farm track, signed: 'No through road'. To the right of the track is a

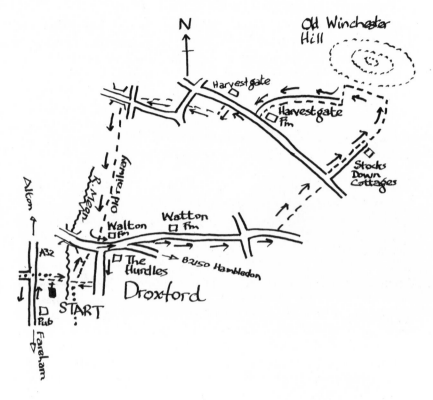

prominent long barrow and to the left a delightful brick and flint shepherd's shelter, complete with chimney. Ahead looms Old Winchester Hill, its summit wreathed by the earthworks of an Iron Age hillfort, its sheep-grazed slopes peppered with juniper bushes. The track passes Stocks Down Cottages on the right and continues as a footpath up to the boundary of the Old Winchester Hill National Nature Reserve (managed by English Nature), with a stile (separate ones for walkers and dogs!) that leads into the reserve. Time to tarry. A notice informs you that: 'This spur of the South Downs is an internationally important chalk downland, sheep grazed to benefit wild flowers and butterflies.' On a clear day the Isle of Wight and the New Forest can be seen from the top of the hill.

Your route turns left and runs for about 400 metres, along a tyre-tracked grassy path that first follows a field boundary on the right and then on the left. It then turns left and heads down a bridleway towards the 'top end' of a coniferous windbreak, where it turns right and descends to a farm (Harvestgate Farm) on a minor road. Turn right onto the road and after 300 metres turn left onto a footpath opposite a house (Harvestgate). This proceeds half-right across a field to a stile in the shadow of a chalk spur (apparently unnamed), where it turns right to follow a field boundary on the left. It crosses a minor road and continues across a grassy field, with houses and bungalows to the left, to a stile at the top, where it traverses a crop field to emerge near a crossroads. Proceed along the road in a westerly direction and after 100 metres reach a bridge of the former Meon valley railway line. Steps descend to the track on the far right-hand side of the bridge. Turn right at the bottom of the steps and continue back to The Hurdles.

For about a kilometre, via alternating causeways and ivy-carpeted, fern-strewn cuttings, the path runs in a southerly direction. When there is a clear view of The Hurdles to the left, descend a path to the B2150. The route continues towards Soberton along Station Road, on the right-hand side of which will be found a pillar box with an inscription, stating that in a special train at this station Winston Churchill spent some days making crucial decisions with his staff, prior to D-Day in 1944. The station alongside the pillar box is now a private dwelling. After 500 metres the route turns right on a bridleway that crosses back over the former railway and proceeds via a kissing-gate to meet the outward path that you followed from Droxford church.

WW The Wayfarer's Walk – Droxford, Soberton and beyond to the 'cradle of cricket' (4 miles)

The 'cradle of cricket' is, of course, Hambledon, where the national game was first played seriously on Broadhalfpenny Down. In more recent years its vineyard and winepress are well known for playing a leading role in the post-war resurgence of English wine. The Wayfarer's Walk reaches this delightful village via Droxford and Soberton, alongside the meadows of the river Meon, and then continues over open countryside and by copses to descend from East Hoe Manor along a woodland path through Lithey's Hanger.

[15] Soberton
The White Lion

Lucy has long been a customer at the White Lion, slipping in for a quick one and . . . er . . . moving round the pictures. The locals have got used to her by now, though they can't find out why she behaves so strangely. Ghosts, it seems, always keep their secrets. But the real secret of the White Lion is, however, its home-cooked food, including delicious warming soups, casseroles, lentil stews, vegetable bakes and goulashes. There are also fast foods, a variety of ploughman's lunches and roast meals on Sundays. As well as the main bar there is a lounge bar with an eating area. A restaurant runs along the back of the pub, which has both a patio and a lawned garden.

The pub offers several real ales, together with Gales country wines, a moderately priced wine list and draught cider. Dogs are welcome in the bar and the landlord is not averse to one eating one's own sandwiches with a drink from the pub in the garden.

The opening times are 11 am to 3 pm (2.30 pm closing in winter) and 6 pm to 11 pm, Monday to Friday. On Saturday the times are 11 am to 11 pm (winter times, 11 am to 4 pm and 6.30 pm to 11 pm)

and on Sunday 12 noon to 10.30 pm (winter times, 12 noon to 4 pm and 7.30 pm to 10.30 pm). Food is served from 12 noon to 2 pm every lunchtime and from opening time to 9.15 pm in the evening.
Telephone: 01489 877346.

How to get there: Soberton is a small village situated less than a mile to the east of the A32 Alton to Fareham road, 7 miles north of Fareham. The White Lion is close to the church.

Parking: There is plenty of parking on the roads around the pub.

Length of the walk: 4½ miles. Map: OS Landranger 185 Winchester and Basingstoke (inn GR 609168).

A walk which traces the river Meon back to Droxford and then climbs up the western slopes of the valley to meet the Wayfarer's Walk. It then runs round the foot of one of those steep bowls – almost a natural amphitheatre – that are typical of chalk downlands, before returning to the comfort of the valley bottom.

The Walk
Walk towards the church and take a path to the left, over a stile. It curls around the outside of the churchyard and then strikes down a field to another stile alongside a minor road by a deep cutting of the former Meon Valley Railway. To the right are the turrets of Soberton Towers. Turn left onto the road: you are now on the route of the Wayfarer's Walk. Cross the railway bridge (Cutts Arch) and turn right at a stile by a bridge over the river Meon (Point A). A path runs towards Droxford, with the river running parallel to it some distance to the left. It passes through a small grove of horse chestnut trees, over a stile, and through sweet meadowland, with Droxford church visible ahead. The path crosses two more stiles, touching the river at the second. Fifty metres further on, at another stile, the path turns left over two footbridges in succession and then passes through a kissing-gate into Droxford churchyard. The path curls round the right-hand side of the church and passes a Wayfarer's Walk sign – 19 miles to Emsworth, 51 miles to Inkpen Beacon.
The route continues ahead, crosses the A32 and heads up Park Lane, opposite the church. It then turns right (leaving the

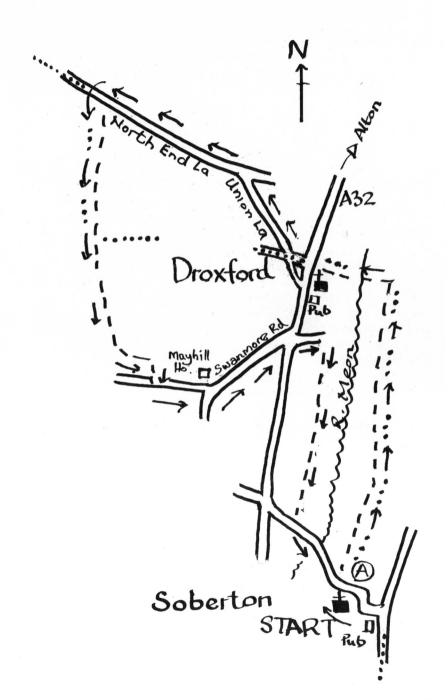

N

North End La

Union La

Alton

A32

Droxford

Pub

Swanmore Rd.

Mayhill Ho.

R. Meon

Ⓐ

Soberton

START

Pub

Wayfarer's Walk for a while) along Union Lane, past a monkey puzzle tree, to a T-junction, where it turns left along North End Lane, signed to Bishop's Waltham and Alresford. The walk climbs, with fine views of Beacon Hill to the north and Old Winchester Hill behind. Where the road levels out on a bend, the route turns **WW** left over a stile and onto a farm track, rejoining the Wayfarer's Walk.

After about 100 metres the path continues over a stile to the left of a field gate and follows the left-hand edge of a field. It dog-legs, then after 100 metres dog-legs again and crosses a stile. It follows the left-hand side of another field and runs into a small copse. At the far side of the copse it meets a stile, with a path straight ahead and another turning in a southerly direction to the right. Follow the latter route, along the edge of a field, turning left at a corner and passing under a steep slope. Where the slope becomes wooded the path turns sharp right, up the western edge of the trees and reaches a tiny single-track lane at the top. The route turns left and follows the lane to meet a T-junction alongside Mayhill House. Turning left down Swanmore Road leads back to the A32. Cross this busy road to a fingerpost pointing down a track and after about 50 metres turn right along a footpath that leads in a southerly direction along the valley. It crosses a stile by a house, with views of the river Meon to the left, and then passes over another stile by a small copse. It emerges at a cottage alongside the minor road we met early in the walk; turning left returns to Point A above, via another small river bridge, and so back to the pub.

[16] Hambledon
The George Hotel

Jazz and summer evenings is the classic mix that the George Hotel brings to this corner of Hampshire on many occasions in the holiday months. Barbecues are also one of its specialities. It is a far cry from days gone by, when this Georgian-style hostelry, whose records date from 1564 (brewing first noted in 1668) was a coaching inn. Stagecoaches joined the Portsmouth to London run at Petersfield. Today, as well as having one large bar inside, there is a coffee bar outside in the courtyard, which is open between 9 am and 11 am. Beers include a range of real ales and there is also draught cider and a good selection of wines. The menu includes bar snacks, à la carte dishes and roasts. Dogs are welcome.

During the summer the coffee bar at the George is open from 9 am to 11 am and the pub from 11 am to 11.30 pm, Monday to Saturday, and 12 noon to 10.30 pm on Sunday. Winter hours are 12 noon to 2.30 pm and 6 pm to 11.30 pm, Monday to Saturday, and 12 noon to 4 pm and 7 pm to 10.30 pm on Sunday. Food is served from 12 noon to 3.30 pm (2 pm in winter) and 6 pm to 10.30 pm (10 pm on Sunday and Monday to Saturday in winter).

Telephone: 01705 632318.

How to get there: Hambledon is about 6 miles north of Portsmouth. It is reached via the B2150, which turns west off the A3 at Waterlooville. The George Hotel is almost opposite the church, in the main street of the village.

Parking: There is plenty of parking at the pub.

Length of the walk: 4 miles. Map: OS Landranger 196 Solent and the Isle of Wight (inn GR 648151).

The hills around Hambledon rise up steeply to level tops. It was on one of these, Broadhalfpenny Down, that the English national game of cricket first came to prominence. This walk touches the famous Hambledon Vineyard and then takes to the hills to the east, before heading down to the village once more and then climbing up to the west. Ever-changing views are lost in the penultimate leg, which winds down through the lovely woodlands of Lithey's Hanger.

The Walk
From the George Hotel walk up towards the church and turn right in front of the church into a sleepy little lane that bends round to the left. A short distance ahead, in front of the local infants school, turn right at a fingerpost onto a path that soon splits in two. Take the right-hand limb and follow a field boundary in an easterly direction. It emerges after a few hundred metres onto a drive on the edge of Hambledon Vineyard (a pioneering venture in the revival of English wine, no longer open to the public). Here the route turns right along the drive, which dog-legs left and right to meet the road through the village. Turn left and immediately right, into a small road that soon forks, the major part turning to the right. Take the left-hand fork and climb steadily for 600 or 700 metres on an old road between steep banks. There are fine views to the left, across to Old Winchester Hill.

The road enters a beech wood and then meets another small road at a T-junction. Here the route turns right into a cul-de-sac and, 100 metres ahead, a track leads off it in a southerly direction beside a large oak tree, whilst the road (to Glidden Farm) turns away to the

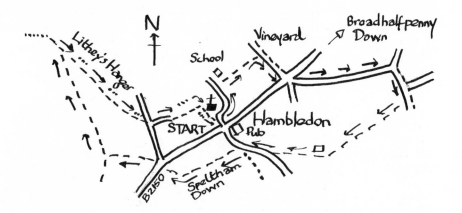

left. About 50 metres along the track a path turns off to the right, under a power line. It continues towards a stile beside a farm building. There are, in fact, two stiles close together. The path proceeds alongside the building, then turns right over a stile and briefly follows the access drive to the property before turning off half-right through a kissing-gate alongside a paddock. It heads downhill between old hedges to meet a lane. The route turns right at a fingerpost and follows the lane, with the village of Hambledon laid out below. Half-way down the lane, beside a house called Dalkeith, two footpaths lead off to the left through a kissing-gate and run across Speltham Down, which belongs to the National Trust. The upper path is on the route of the Wayfarer's Walk, but we take the lower path, which runs in a south-westerly direction.

At the far side of the path, under a telephone line, it passes through a kissing-gate and turns right to meet the B2150. Turn right and, after 100 metres, reach once more the road through the village, which forks off to the right. At this junction, turn left at a fingerpost on the opposite side of the B2150, alongside the nameplate 'Green Lane', where a narrow path runs between houses. It climbs uphill and forks; we take the right-hand limb and continue climbing. The footpath quickly bends to the right, passes over a stile and heads in a northerly direction along the edge of a wood, and then into the heart of the same wood at a stile, alongside several old pits. Wonderful! At the far side of the wood the route continues through a long thin copse, with a field falling away to the right. It reaches a stile, where the Wayfarer's Walk heads off across a field in a north-westerly direction, with East Hoe Manor ahead.

WW Our route now follows the long-distance walk back to the village. Turn back at an acute angle and walk in a south-easterly direction, downhill across the 'falling away' field, to its bottom left-hand corner, where a stile leads back into the wood near a small pit. A path leads through the wood, with the steep slope of Lithey's Hanger to the left, and descends to meet the B2150 at a fingerpost. Here the route dog-legs right and left and continues across Stewart's Green at right angles to the road. It passes between houses towards Hambledon church, where it goes through a kissing-gate beside a high wall and then turns right to pass the west end of the church, and so back to the George.

WW The Wayfarer's Walk – Hambledon to Denmead (2 miles)
The great conurbation of Portsmouth and Southsea lurks not far away from Hambledon, though the leg onwards to Denmead is remote, with few signs of the 20th century. These lands were taken into cultivation from the huge Forest of Bere that once stretched east from this part of Hampshire, notably after 1810, when the forest was the subject of an official enclosure.

[17] Denmead
The White Hart

Close to the tiny village green, in the fork of the roads from Hambledon and Southwick, the White Hart has been in every sense at the centre of Denmead life for a very long time. Some say it has been a pub since the beginning of the 18th century. Today, it is a thoroughly modern-style hostelry owned by Surrey Free Inns. There is one very large bar, attractively arranged with a variety of seating areas. Outside is a large garden with children's attractions. For evening entertainment, the pub prizes itself on its quizzes. Dogs are not allowed in the bar. It has a branded 'Farmhouse Kitchen' menu, supplemented with a daily specials board and traditional Sunday roasts. It offers a changing panel of real ales and a selection of reasonably priced wines.

The opening times during the summer are likely to be 'all day, every day', but they are more restricted in the winter, namely, 11 am to 2.30 pm and 6 pm to 11.30 pm Monday to Saturday, and 12 noon to 3 pm and 7 pm to 10.30 pm on Sunday. Meals are served from 12 noon to 2 pm and 6.30 pm to 9.30 pm (10 pm on Saturday) and 12 noon to 2.30 pm and 7 pm to 9 pm on Sunday.

Telephone: 01705 255953.

How to get there: Denmead is on the B2150, 4 miles north of Portsmouth. It is reached by turning west off the A3 at Waterlooville. The White Hart is on the left, just after an arcade of shops and the village green.

Parking: There is ample parking alongside the pub.

Length of the walk: 3 miles. Map: OS Landranger 196 Solent and the Isle of Wight (inn GR 655121).

One of the most enjoyable features of this part of Hampshire, highlighted by this walk, is that within a few miles of a major city like Portsmouth there still exists an intricate countryside that is essentially Saxon in origin. Several centuries of the Royal Navy may have spoilt the coastline, but inland all is quiet.

The Walk
From the side of the White Hart that fronts the B2150, turn right towards the centre of Denmead and, after 100 metres, bear left at **WW** the tiny village green into Park Road. This is on the Wayfarer's Walk, as indicated by the prominent sign - 'Inkpen Beacon 58'. About 100 metres ahead, just to the right of the 'Rookwood View' nameplate, a footpath leads between houses. Where the houses finish the path turns left, with a cemetery to the right. It curls to the left, behind the houses, passes over a plank bridge and then turns right, heading in a northerly direction towards two high-tension lines. On the left ahead are the woodlands of Antilly Common and Forest Gate, and beyond can be seen Rookwood Farm. This is an ancient site; the building has traces of Norman work, including an undercroft. The route continues ahead, ignoring turnings right and left, towards the further power line. It meets a country road, at a point several hundred metres to the right of the farm, and turns left and almost immediately right at a T-junction, along a tiny road. The Wayfarer's Walk soon turns off to the left, across fields, towards Hambledon.
Continue along the road to a small crossroads, with the Bat and Ball pub (famous in cricketing circles) signposted ahead and Denmead to the right. Turn right along the road and almost

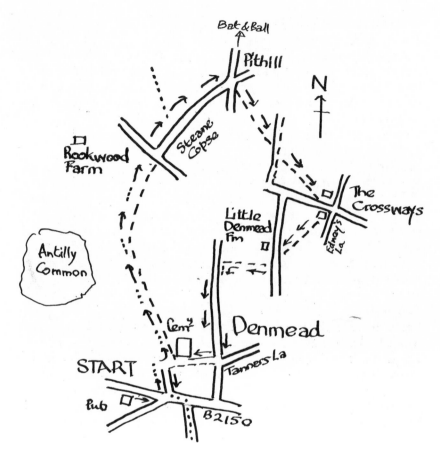

immediately take a footpath that slips off to the left and runs in a
south-easterly direction, up a steep slope to the left of a pylon. It
reaches a stile in a hedge and continues in the same direction (140°
magnetic) across the corner of a crop field, towards another pylon
beyond a line of trees. (Be bold! Fight for the footpaths of
England!) The path crosses another stile at a bridleway and
continues ahead towards a white house beside a pylon, meeting a
minor road at a fingerpost, just to the right of the house. Our route
turns left onto the road and meets a staggered T-junction beside the
house, where we turn right and then, at the far side of the house,
turn right again at the 'Edney's Lane' nameplate.

Hereafter, cross a crop field in a south-westerly direction

towards a farmhouse with a corrugated iron roof (Little Denmead Farm). Here the path meets a farm road, where we turn left and then right along the far side of Bleak Cottage, at a stile and fingerpost. The path continues via several stiles to the corner of a field, where it turns left along a hedge to a stile leading to a minor road. Turn left along the road, with views to the right of the houses in Rookwood View where the walk started. After a few hundred metres, where Tanner's Lane comes in from the left, a path turns right along Cemetery Lane and leads back to the start.

WW The Wayfarer's Walk – Denmead to Purbrook Heath (3 miles)
From Denmead the Wayfarer's Walk passes by Denmead Pottery, well known for its ceramic products, and then takes a delightful route across countryside that lies in the lee of Portsdown Hill, This great chalk fold keeps all the bustling activity of Portsmouth out of view, in an area where the pleasures of the woods and the fields have not succumbed to the town. The walk passes the entrance to Purbrook Heath House, formerly Southwick House, although the village from which it got its name lies 2 miles to the west. The original Southwick House in Southwick itself is now occupied by HMS *Dryad*.

[18] Southwick
The Golden Lion

Southwick is one of those rare villages that is owned by one person, namely Mr Robin Thistlethwaite. He lives in Oxfordshire and spends only a couple of days each week on his estates, which he inherited a few years ago. Despite its 500-year age tag, none of this 'feudalism' is apparent in the Golden Lion, which is one of the best pubs for a long way. It certainly impressed Eisenhower and Montgomery during the last war, for they took it over at the time of D-Day and spread out maps in the bar. 'Not very secure,' I hear you say; but the pub was protected by military police and was open to no one else! The generals were there because the headquarters for Operation Overlord, of which D-Day was a part, were in the original Southwick House (now occupied by HMS *Dryad*). The plans still hang in the wardroom. The ancestral family moved to another Southwick House (now called Purbrook Heath House) built 2 miles to the east on Purbrook Heath.

The pub is a freehouse and serves mainly Courage beers. There is a large lounge bar and a rear snug, together with a restaurant area. The menu is varied, from sandwiches to steaks, with Sunday roasts.

Dogs are allowed in the bar on a lead. The car park contains a rare example of an early 19th- century brewhouse, which can be viewed by appointment (telephone: 01705 380978).

The opening times in the summer are 11 am to 2.30 pm and 6 pm to 11 pm Monday to Saturday (winter, 12 noon to 2.30 pm and 7 pm to 11 pm) and 12 noon to 3 pm and 7 pm to 10.30 pm on Sunday.
Telephone: 01705 379134

How to get there: Southwick is situated off the A333 between Wickham and Cosham and is easily reached from junction 12 of the M27 or from the A3. The pub lies just beyond a turning to the right to HMS *Dryad*.

Parking: There is a large car park behind the pub and another adjacent car park owned by the parish council.

Length of the walk: 5 miles, with shorter walks of 3 miles (see text, Point A) and 4 miles (Point B). Map: OS Landranger 196 Solent and the Isle of Wight (inn GR 627085).

Only a small part of the Wayfarer's Walk is included in this walk, in the vicinity of Sheepwash Farm. The circular route passes through a varied landscape of woods and open fields, and for part of its route follows the course of the river Wallington, which reaches the sea at Fareham.

The Walk
From the Golden Lion turn right and walk past the church and the Red Lion, along the road to Denmead. After about 500 metres, just beyond modern houses (Boulter Lane), a footpath turns right at a fingerpost and runs along a wall on the right. It enters trees, immediately turns sharp left and then winds its way through a plantation of sweet chestnut. It becomes a track, which keeps ahead at the meeting of five tracks, and then crosses another, rougher, track, before continuing ahead amongst young beech and oak trees littered with enormous stumps. This part of the route is rather sinuous but is easily followed with the aid of yellow-topped marker poles. The woodland path bends round to the left, through a patch of broom, and then comes to a stile on the right. The route cuts half-left across the corner of a field to another stile and then turns

86

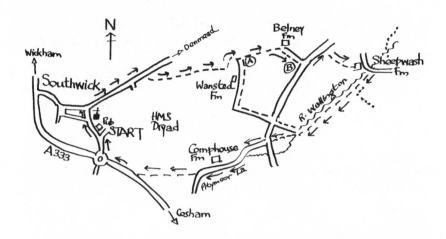

right and runs for a short distance between fences. The route meets a track (if you want a shorter walk, turn right here – see sketch map, Point A), where it turns left for 50 metres and then right over a stile alongside a field gate. The path continues over a field, making for the left-hand edge of a wood ahead, where it meets an apology of a stile beside a gate.

It then heads towards a corrugated iron cattle shed (Belney Farm), to the left of which is another stile. Turn right, along the access drive of the farm, which curls to the right to meet a country road. The route turns left (turning right is another short cut – see sketch map, Point B) along the road, with woodland on the left, and after a few hundred metres turns right between two houses, at a fingerpost. The path enters a yard and then continues straight ahead via several stiles, eventually skirting Sheepwash Farm. Here it meets a minor road, where it turns right, crosses the river Wallington and then turns right again, downstream. We are now, briefly, on the **WW** Wayfarer's Walk, which turns off to the left after a few hundred metres, at Kerry's Post, which commemorates 'an intrepid little Yorkie'.

The path continues along a delightful track through woodland, with occasional glimpses of the river, which flows parallel to it to the right. After emerging from the wood, with the river still to the right, the route crosses a footbridge where three footpaths meet at a ford. It turns left on a footpath that slips under the railings of the bridge and soon moves away from the river bank to head in a roughly westerly direction. It crosses a field to meet minor roads at a T-junction. The route continues straight ahead for about 500 metres, along the leg of the T. It winds round to pass Comphouse Farm and soon after, where the road (Pitymoor Lane) takes a sharp bend to the left, a footpath turns off to the right at a fingerpost. It proceeds in a westerly direction, along the boundary wall of HMS *Dryad* (formerly Southwick House and before that Southwick Priory) to meet the busy A333. Turning right returns to Southwick, via wide verges and a convenient slip road. Turn right at the roundabout at the entrance to the village, to return to the Golden Lion.

WW The Wayfarer's Walk – Purbrook Heath House to Langstone (6 miles)

From Purbrook Heath House, which is 2 miles east of Southwick village, the route of the Wayfarer's Walk runs east to connect with a path on the edge of Purbrook Heath. This heads south to Widley, where the route flirts with the A3 before following the slightly quieter B2177. This road continues along the top of Portsdown Hill, a ridge of chalk that provides superb views of Portsmouth and its harbour. The route circles round Fort Purbrook, one of six forts built after 1860, at the time of Napoleon III, to protect Portsmouth from possible encircling attacks by the French approaching from the north. Ordered by Palmerston, the Prime Minister of the day, they were never required and have been dubbed, perhaps somewhat unfairly, as 'Palmerston's Follies'. The Wayfarer's Walk has now to negotiate the industrial landscape of Bedhampton (where it meets the Solent Way), but it soon drops down to the foreshore at the top of Langstone Harbour and heads east to Langstone, a pretty waterside village that is, in fact, at the head of Chichester Harbour.

[19] Langstone
The Royal Oak

One of the finest shoreside pubs in the south, the Royal Oak looks out across Chichester Harbour to Hayling Island. It once served the sailors who brought corn to the windmill alongside, which is now a private residence. Today, the pub is well patronised, amongst others, by yachties, who sail up for a pint at high water. It is said to date from the 16th century, and, like most old pubs, it has a wealth of history and legend. With scarce a smile, you will be told of a hidden room upstairs, of tales of smugglers, of a tunnel that leads to the mill, of a lady ghost . . . and much else. It was even a royal refuge – Charles the something or was it George? – why else would it be called the *Royal* Oak? But beware: the last laugh may be on the landlord!

The food is all home-cooked and includes plenty of fish dishes. Blackboard specials and French sticks are a regular feature. Beers include Marston's Pedigree and a changing list of real ales. A good selection of wines is on offer. There is one bar with a separate food area and a garden outside. Dogs are welcome in the main bar.

The opening times are 11 am to 11 pm Monday to Saturday and

12 noon to 10.30 pm on Sunday. Food is available from 12 noon to 9.30 pm.
Telephone: 01705 483125.

How to get there: From the A27 south of Havant, turn south on the A3023 road to Langstone and Hayling Island. After about half a mile, just past a yellow-painted weather-boarded house, turn left into Langstone High Street. The Royal Oak is round the left-hand corner at the seaward end.

Parking: There is limited parking in Langstone High Street, but it would be courteous to local residents to park instead in the public car park nearby, situated on the east side of the north end of the bridge to Hayling Island. Instead of turning into Langstone High Street, continue for about 100 metres on the A3023 and turn left into the car park, which is alongside the Ship Inn.

Length of the walk: 4 miles, in two 'sectors' (see text), each of which makes about 2 miles and can be walked separately. Map: OS Landranger 197 Chichester and The Downs (inn GR 720049).

This walk explores the coast at the north end of Langstone and Chichester Harbours. Here, amidst the tangle of roads that has grown up in recent times, are the vestiges of an earlier age, when mills turned by tide-lapped shores. The walk passes through Warblington, a charming village that was almost, but not quite, swallowed by urban sprawl.

The Walk
There are two distinct sectors to this walk. The first explores the shore at the top of Langstone Harbour to the west and the second that of Chichester Harbour to the east. Note that Langstone is not in Langstone Harbour! It is a pretty seaside village (albeit prone to flooding at high water) on the edge of urban sprawl. *The first sector* starts by retracing Langstone High Street back to the A3023, or if you are in the car park beside the A3023, alongside the Ship Inn, walk north to the entrance to Langstone High Street. Across the road, slightly to the right is a footpath by a telephone box, with a lovely laid hedge on the left. It passes a Wayfarer's Walk sign (Inkpen Beacon 67½, Emsworth 2½) and soon meets a cul-de-sac

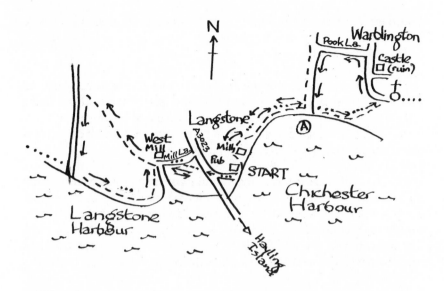

(Mill Lane), where the route turns left and continues down to the end. Here stands West Mill (presumably 'east mill' is the old windmill at Langstone), still surrounded by streams and situated on the banks of a narrow tidal inlet.

The path crosses the inlet to a stile and continues across marshy ground in a north-westerly direction, passing just to the left of power lines, with a large garish factory with green trimmings some distance away to the right. It crosses a plank bridge and comes to a stile at footpath signs, with four distinct paths leading from the far side. Take the right-hand path, which runs alongside a hedge, marked with prominent blue footpath signs. It bends to the left and passes between hedges to a road, where the route turns left to the sea, to reach a small car park. There are fine views of the top of Langstone Harbour, which is dotted with small islands, including Long Island and North Binness Island. The route now turns left along the foreshore, back to the tidal inlet, where it turns left again to return to West Mill. Approaching from this direction the rushing millstream of West Mill can still be clearly seen emerging from under the garden wall. The route returns to Langstone High Street, which is a conservation area. The left-hand side of the street presents a charming façade of simple flat-fronted cottages, some thatched and said to date from the 16th century.

Sandbags and watertight bulkheads tell their own story, for at high water these houses risk being flooded. To the right is the chapel of St Nicholas, a small church attached to Langstone Towers, a private house with a distinctive eight-dormered tower.

The second sector of the walk starts at the seaward end of Langstone High Street, where it turns left past the Royal Oak. Ahead is the Old Mill, formerly a windmill used to grind corn brought here by sea. The black stump of the mill stands amidst a jumble of red-brick extensions with balconies overlooking the water. It was the Petersfield artist Flora Twort who bought and restored the mill in 1932. The path passes behind the mill, past a reedy millpond, now a bird sanctuary, which was recently cleaned and restored. The path continues along the foreshore, a large part of which is protected by a wall of railway sleepers. Ahead is the steeple of Warblington church and the broken tower of Warblington Castle. The path passes a seat near a rectangular array of what old maps show was a quay (Point A).

When abreast of the castle, the route turns inland and passes through a cemetery to the 13th-century church, which stands on Saxon foundations. The Wayfarer's Walk and the Solent Way continue ahead. Our route turns back, with the cemetery on the left, and follows the road round to the right. It passes a fine malmstone house which stands on the right, at the entrance to Warblington House. From this point there is a good view of the ruins of Warblington Castle, but the grounds are private. Just ahead on the left is a memorial seat to Eline Morgan (1920-88). Ahead the A27 thunders on, but we turn left down Pook Lane, a cul-de-sac. We pass The Old Rectory, a fine five-bay Georgian house, and at the end of the lane turn left along a lovely track that runs between high banks. Presumably it once served the castle and the quay . . . if only banks could talk! It leads back to Point A and so back to the Royal Oak, with picture postcard views of Langstone.

WW **The Wayfarer's Walk – Langstone to Emsworth (2 miles)**
The last leg! And navigation could not be simpler. The path heads east along the foreshore to Warblington, where it turns inland and proceeds to Nore Barn Open Space to the west of Emsworth. Here it regains the foreshore and continues to Emsworth, where it runs around the edge of the millpond of a former tide mill, now the premises of the Emsworth Slipper Sailing Club and the termination of the Wayfarer's Walk. All good things must end!

[20] Emsworth
The Blue Bell

If you can tell the landlord how this pub acquired its name (definitely not the Bluebell) you may get a free pint. The present building only dates from 1953, although a pub is believed to have existed on this site for a long time. It is strange that in a town like Emsworth, with one of the most interesting shorelines in the south, there is no pub that looks over the water. The Blue Bell is the nearest pub to the shore and what it lacks in views it more than makes up for in other respects.

Its menu includes home-cooked fish dishes with locally caught fresh fish, with a specials board every day. It is a freehouse serving Ruddles Best and a guest real ale, as well as a number of carefully chosen house wines – the landlord likes a glass or two himself! Dogs are welcome in the bar. There are two patio areas outside the pub.

The opening times are from 11 am to 11 pm Monday to Saturday and 12 noon to 10.30 pm on Sunday. Meals are served from 12 noon to 2.30 pm and 6 pm to 10 pm Monday to Saturday and 12 noon to 2.15 pm and 7 pm to 9 pm on Sunday, except on Sunday evenings in winter.

Telephone: 01243 373394.

How to get there: From the A27 Portsmouth to Chichester road take the A259 into the centre of Emsworth and turn right into South Street. Just beyond the Blue Bell pub, half-way down on the right, turn right into a public car park.

Parking: There is plenty of room in the pay and display car park alongside the Blue Bell, though it tends to get full at peak shopping times. There are no charges after 5 pm on Saturday and none at all on Sunday and Bank Holidays.

Length of the walk: 3 miles. Map: OS Landranger 197 Chichester and The Downs (inn GR 747056).

A walk that explores the western side of Emsworth's harbour and foreshore, at the head of the Emsworth Channel of Chichester Harbour. It reaches Warblington and then returns by a slightly different route.

The Walk
Walk down South Street to Town Quay, which is the start of both the Wayfarer's Walk and the Solent Way. On the quay is an old tide mill, now the premises of the Emsworth Slipper Sailing Club, its initials wittily picked out on the east wall with the end plates of reinforcing rods. Emsworth was a busy port until the turn of the century, when the local oyster fisheries were killed by sewage and, coincidentally, milling declined. The walk starts by running round the edge of the former millpond, which was bought by the Warblington Urban District Council in 1925, the sea wall being built at the personal expense of its chairman, Mr Nöel Kinnels. In the summer the pond is a venue for watersports and carnivals. Half-way round on the left is a public jetty, built in 1995 to provide access to the main channel. Note also the stumps of a fisherman's walkway which can be seen at low water; it led to oysteries in one of the channels (Fowley Rythe) and can still be walked for some way. The mudflats hereabouts are seething with waders and other sea birds, so numerous that they sometimes look like greenfly on a rose bush.
   At the far side of the pond the path passes to the right of

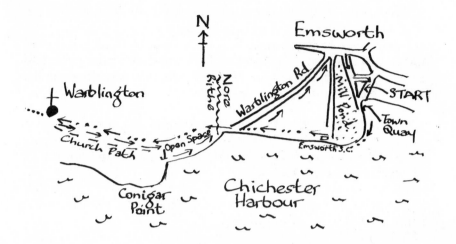

Emsworth Sailing Club and runs between walls to the western promenade. Ahead is the wooded outline of Conigar Point and, in the distance to the left, the bridge that connects Hayling Island to the mainland. The route continues along a gravel road beside the sea (Western Parade), crosses a small stream (Nore Rithe) on the edge of the town and starts to head inland and pass through woodland along the right-hand edge of Nore Barn Open Space, along Church Path. It passes through two kissing-gates and continues in a westerly direction to Warblington, with a hedge on the left. Ahead is the village church, with the ruined tower of Warblington Castle to the right. It passes a large cemetery on the left and then turns through a kissing-gate into the east end of the churchyard. Just inside is a Gothic-style gravewatcher's hut, once used to deter local 'Jekyll and Hydes'! There are a number of interesting graves, including that of William Palmer, who 'lost his life and vessel going into Dublin' in 1750 (or is it 1759?), which faces out from the south-east corner of the church. The scene is depicted in relief at the top of the stone.

The walk now retraces the route back to the western edge of the Nore Barn woods, where it turns right and heads towards a seat beside the sea. To the left in the distance can be seen Thorney Island, which since 1870 has in fact been joined to the mainland. Between 1938 and 1976 it contained an RAF base. The walk now continues along the foreshore, recrosses Nore Rithe on the edge of the town and turns left along a residential road (Warblington Road) that heads diagonally inland. It briefly touches the main road, where it turns right and then crosses the head of the millpond and turns right again down Bridgefoot Path, which runs down the east side of the pond. Half-way down, Nile Street turns off to the left and runs back to the centre of Emsworth and so back to the car park. It is an example of Shurlock's Law: All walks start and end at a car park. Let's hope you didn't leave your lights on!

Hampshire County Council

The council's rights of way department manages and maintains over 3,500 kilometres of footpaths, bridleways and byways in Hampshire. The council has developed seven long-distance walks in Hampshire, including the Wayfarer's Walk. It also produces a range of publications to encourage the public to explore Hampshire by using this network. (For more details, contact their information centre on 01962 870500).

Tourist Information Centres

Andover – Town Mill House, Bridge Street, Hants SP10 1BL
(tel: 01264 324320)

Basingstoke – Willis Museum, Old Town Hall, Hants RG21 1QD
(tel: 01256 817618)

Havant – 1 Park Road South, Hants PO9 1HA
(tel: 01705 480024)

Newbury – The Wharf, Berks RG14 5AS
(tel: 01635 30267)

Petersfield – County Library, 27 The Square, Hants GU32 3HH
(tel: 01730 268829)

Winchester – The Guildhall, The Broadway, Hants SO23 9LJ
(tel: 01962 841365)